# PERFECT MARKETS AND EASY VIRTUE

T0327466

𝕁𝔹

# Mitsui Lectures in Economics

*Series Editor:* L. Alan Winters, University of Birmingham

Money and Inflation
*Frank Hahn*

# Perfect Markets and Easy Virtue

*Business Ethics and
the Invisible Hand*

*William J. Baumol, with
Sue Anne Batey Blackman*

BLACKWELL
Cambridge MA & Oxford UK

First published 1991

Blackwell Publishers
Three Cambridge Center
Cambridge, Massachusetts 02142, USA

108 Cowley Road, Oxford, OX4 1JF, UK

*Library of Congress Cataloging in Publication Data*
Baumol, William J.
Perfect markets and easy virtue: business ethics and the invisible hand/
William J. Baumol with Sue Anne Batey Blackman.
p. cm. – (Mitsui lectures in economics)
Includes bibliographical references and index.
ISBN 1-55786-248-6
1. Capitalism – Moral and ethical aspects. 2. Business ethics.
3. Competition – Moral and ethical aspects. 4. Industry – Social
aspects. 5. Prices – Government policy. I. Blackman, Sue Anne
Batey. II. Title. III. Series.
HB501 . B372 1991
174'.4–dc20                                                   91-16775
                                                                CIP

*British Library Cataloguing in Publication Data*

A CIP catalogue record for this book is available from the British Library.

Typeset in $10\frac{1}{2}$ on $13\frac{1}{2}$ pt Palatino
by Graphicraft Typesetters Ltd, Hong Kong

This book is printed on acid-free paper.

# Contents

# *Preface*

This little book has its origins in the invitation to the senior author ("senior" in number of years of survival) to deliver the 1990 Mitsui Lectures at the University of Birmingham. This very distinguished lecture series clearly called for a good deal more than mere recycling of some standard talk that the speaker keeps put away in the file cabinet to be pulled out once again for the next stop on the lecture circuit.

The timing of the lectures suggested their topic. The centrally planned economies of Eastern Europe had just broken away from domination by the Soviet Union and from the supposedly Marxist principles that guided the workings of their economies. Recourse to the market mechanism became the cliché that was used to characterize the new direction toward which they aspired to turn.

But there were disturbing signs that many inhabitants of those countries were not aware of what the market mechanism entails and what circumstances are necessary for it to perform the miracles that Karl Marx admired so extravagantly: "It has accomplished wonders far surpassing Egyptian pyramids, Roman aqueducts and Gothic cathedrals. . . . The bourgeoisie, during its rule of scarce one hundred years, has created more massive and more colossal productive forces than all previous generations together" (*The Communist Manifesto*). They seemed unwilling to recognize that the market mechanism depends for its effectiveness upon the pursuit of self-interest – upon unmitigated greed – and that rules imposing extreme equality of income consequently are likely to undermine its workings and to prevent it from generating that flow of economic abundance which is its saving grace. As Adam Smith put the point, "by directing . . . industry in such a manner as its produce may be of the greatest value, [the individual] intends only his own gain, and he is in this, as in many other cases, led by an invisible hand to promote that which was no part of his intention" (*Wealth of Nations*, Book IV, Chapter II). Inescapably, the market mechanism also has what many would regard as its dark sides, which do not vanish even when the market assumes the forms that constitute its theoretical ideal (perfect competition or perfect contestability).

The object adopted for the Mitsui Lectures was, accordingly, to explore those dark sides, seeking to outline them explicitly and to bring them fully into the open. For, surely, unless those less lovable aspects of its workings are understood fully, a dispassionate evaluation is impossible, and the adoption of a market regime is certain to elicit discontent and disillusion along with the flow of wealth that it provides. Along with this exploration of the less attractive attributes of the market, the lectures were intended to provide examples of some of its workings that would seem to achieve surprisingly commendable performance and to describe uses of the market mechanism in which it becomes an effective tool for ameliorating its own deficiencies. Thus, the discussion sought sedulously to avoid advocacy either against or on behalf of the market mechanism. Rather, it undertook to describe, more or less dispassionately, some of its less widely recognized powers to promote the social welfare, along with all the accompanying warts and blemishes.

Not that we ourselves are uncommitted in our own views. It is only fair to admit to the reader that our own pre-conceptions do strongly favor reliance on the market and upon market instruments, but only after substantial inter-vention to correct some of their most damaging defects. No doubt that point of view emerges rather clearly in the third of the three essays in this book. That last lecture, which was added to the original Mitsui Lectures, is the product of the partnership of the two authors of this volume. It is a partnership, it should be added, that has endured for many years, to our mutual pleasure, and which, we trust, will go on for many more.

Finally, we must express our deep thanks to the Price Institute for Entrepreneurial Studies and the C. V. Starr Center for Applied Economics for their generous support of this work, and to Elizabeth Bailey and Robert Willig for their very useful comments on portions of the manuscript.

William J. Baumol and Sue Anne Batey Blackman
Princeton, New Jersey
February 1991

# 1

# (Almost) Perfect Competition (Contestability) and Business Ethics

## William J. Baumol*

The subject of the invisible-hand theorem in the *Wealth of Nations* is a businessperson who is virtuous in spite of himself. The market mechanism forces him to serve the general welfare in order to pursue his own interests. Moreover, "By pursuing his own interest he frequently promotes that of the society more effectually than when he really intends to promote it" (*Wealth of Nations*, invisible-hand passage). The point is that businesspeople are only human, so their moral propensities span the range from impeccability to untrustworthiness, exactly like those of

* I am well aware that, like a joke that telegraphs its punch line, the conclusions in this chapter may become obvious once they are even hinted at. Still, they seem to be reasonably significant, and not generally recognized. Here, as is so often the case, there is a clear exception in the work of Kenneth Arrow, who more than fifteen years ago [1973a and b] dealt effectively with all three topics covered in this chapter, though his orientation was very different from mine.

lawyers, doctors, or professors. The invisible-hand mechanism, as Adam Smith describes it, saves society from dependence on the virtues of any individual "merchant or manufacturer."

But the virtuous performance that the invisible hand ensures is rather restricted. The firm is forced to adapt its output combination to the preferences of consumers, and to use resources with maximal efficiency in producing these outputs. Moreover, as we now know, and as Smith clearly suggested, such allocative efficiency is guaranteed by the market only if it is perfectly competitive (or perfectly contestable).

Many observers who are not professional economists hope the business community will show much more evidence of virtuous behavior than mere allocative efficiency. Three attributes that recur in discussions of good behavior are, first, maintenance of integrity in product quality (avoidance of adulteration and observance of "truth in advertising"); second, voluntary pursuit of social goals (e.g., upholding environmental protection, giving financial support to education, health care, and the arts, or avoiding business activity in countries whose behavior is considered beyond the pale); and third, avoidance of any taint of discrimination in employment by race, sex, or religious affiliation (to distinguish this bias from price discrimination we will refer to it as "social discrimination"). This list may not exhaust the qualities commonly expected of the virtuous businessperson, but it seems at least to cover a considerable part of the range.

Now, one may well suspect that economists generally do not associate perfect competition or contestability with the standards of performance that may be expected of the business community in any of these three areas. That is, those who have not sought to analyze the subject may well be expected to believe that those market forms have no systematic implications, one way or the other, about business performance in terms of the three types of virtue just listed. Under perfect competition, on such a view, whether a firm or industry does well or badly in seeking any or all of those goals is inherently a fortuitous matter, depending on the propensities of the decision makers and a variety of influences other than market form.

The purpose in the first section of this paper is to show that this reading of the matter is inaccurate; indeed, that almost precisely the opposite is true. Under perfect competition or perfect contestability, morality of each of the three types in our list is removed almost entirely from the discretion of the business decision makers. Instead, at least so far as the first two of the three virtues are concerned, business firms are condemned to behave exactly as they do, (almost) regardless of personal preference; and with respect to the third virtue, the market mechanism, at least, makes a considerable difference. In particular, it will be shown that perfection in competition or contestability precludes all genuine business voluntarism, including care for the environment beyond that imposed by law, or voluntary donations to beneficent eleemosynary institutions. Thus, in this arena, these "perfect" market forms impose vice rather than virtue. With respect to product quality and completeness and accuracy of product information, these market forms perform almost as badly, and are likely to provide, perhaps more than any other market forms, both the incentive and the opportunity for product degradation and misrepresentation. (For a very nice discussion of the dangers of quality degradation in contestable markets, see Rashid [1988].) In contrast, the performance of our focal market forms will be exemplary as applied to the third category of business virtue, totally preventing socially discriminatory behavior in employment, in wages, in service to different customer groups, or in any other form.

From all this, I will draw some conclusions about antitrust activity, not seeking to inject the three virtues as proper goals for the antitrust laws, but suggesting that empirical observations of business behavior with respect to these virtues can be used as supplementary evidence of the presence or absence of market power. Finally, I will extend the argument, by analogy, to the implications for market performance of the findings in recent psychologically oriented literature on the economic behavior of individuals. If market forces can preclude businesspersons from exercising their predisposition to vice or virtue, will they similarly circumscribe the influence of other psychological propensities?

Having discussed some static implications of perfect competition and perfect contestability in this chapter, I will turn, in Chapter 2, to some of their intertemporal consequences.

## PRODUCT DEGRADATION AND MISREPRESENTATION

The seminal work of Akerlof [1970], Shapiro [1982, 1983], and others has focused attention on the importance of variations in product quality and imperfections in the pertinent information available to the market. The entire problem associated with pricing and selling items of poor quality whose inferiority is not easily determined by purchasers (the problem posed by products that prove to be "lemons") has become the focus of a rich body of literature. For us, what matters here is the determination of the circumstances in which the supplier will find it possible and profitable to degrade the product, or deliberately to withhold or misrepresent information about it.

It is now recognized that in a market operated by decision

makers who pursue their individual interests, personal morality cannot always be relied upon to prevent misrepresentation or deliberate degrading of products. The underlying principle, which we will generalize later, is that any firm attempting to do so on its own in the presence of unscrupulous rivals is apt to find itself at a severe competitive disadvantage. Consequently, its good behavior will terminate rapidly, either because it is abandoned by management as a matter of self-preservation, or, if management holds out because of its moral convictions, because the ethical firm is driven out of the market altogether, succumbing to the competitive prowess of its less fastidious rivals. In fact, there are markets, such as bazaars that cater largely to transient tourists, in which misrepresentation is indeed the norm of behavior and caveat emptor loses any aura of quaint exaggeration.

What modern analysts have described as the attribute of most markets that prevents matters there from reaching such an unhappy pass is the value of reputation to the seller (see, e.g., Heal [1976]). Several elements contribute a value to reputation: (1) the seller must not be anonymous, and must stand out from the crowd sufficiently to be recognized by customers and distinguished from the others in the field; (2) the seller must have a more lasting commitment to the market, expecting to carry out transactions there the day after tomorrow as well as today; (3) the customers, too, must engage in repeated transactions so that they can inexpensively learn by doing (that is, by purchasing), to distinguish trustworthy from untrustworthy sellers; alternatively, without a substantial body of repeating purchasers, a ready and effective means must be at hand for past customers to communicate to future buyers their degree of satisfaction with the products of a seller and with the treatment they received at that person's hands.

Without a system of enforceable warranties, each of these is a necessary condition for the invisible hand to be effective in ensuring that products are not misrepresented or adulterated; together, the three conditions seem to be sufficient for the purpose. In the absence of any one of them, the unscrupulous seller can escape observation of his behavior, and the consequent irrelevance or total absence of reputation means that nothing (financial) is to be lost by him as a result of cheating his customers. On the other hand, product quality becomes reliable where all three conditions hold – when the seller is noticeable, she depends on repeated sales for her long-run payoff, and customers are in a position to learn, without incurring a large learning cost, that a seller is not to be trusted. In such circumstances, the invisible hand will tend to elicit suitable product quality and information because the punishment for misbehavior on this score will be rapid and will automatically fit the crime.

One useful way of looking at the matter is to recognize that in reality almost all markets are organized as *repeated* games. But although the games are usually repeated, the participants may or may not vary in identity from one play to another. The pertinent distinction, then, is between repeated games in which the players are *enduring* and those in which they are *transient*. The typical payoff matrices for these two cases will differ markedly. Thus, consider the matrix for a typical firm, *T*, in a market of transient players. Even though the game is repeated, the matrix giving the outcome of a single-period play is all that is pertinent to the decision-making process of any agent. If we simplify matters by assuming that the player's decision is a binary choice between misrepresentation (*M*) and honesty (*H*), for the transient-players case we can expect to obtain a payoff matrix such as the following:

Other firms in the market

|  | | M | H |
|---|---|---|---|
| Firm *T* | M | moderate | high |
|  | H | low | moderate |

Payoff Matrix 1: The Transient Players Case

We see that firm *T* can expect to earn what is referred to here as a "moderate" (intermediate) level of profits, which may entail zero economic profits, if it follows the practice of all other sellers in misrepresenting its products. On the other hand, should other sellers set a norm of honesty, firm *T* can earn a high profit by misrepresenting, thereby saving on product-quality costs, and getting away with it before exiting from the market in which its participation is, by hypothesis, not repeated. The logic of the remaining entries in the matrix is sufficiently obvious to require no explanation. But the main point is that for typical firm, *T*, in such circumstances, strategy *M* unambiguously dominates strategy *H*, and this is the manner in which market forces will, in these circumstances, *impose* a regime of misrepresentation and degradation of product quality. Moreover, under the conditions postulated, this outcome is what rational consumers will expect, though they will be powerless to do anything about it, even if they are quite willing to pay the added cost of ensured quality.

Matters are quite different where the players' participation endures, so that they all play repeatedly and for a substantial number of times. Here, collapsing the streams of payoffs from different strategy choices for typical firm *T* into scalar discounted present values, we obtain our second payoff matrix:

Other firms in the market

M          H

|          |   | M | H |
|----------|---|---|---|
| Firm *T* | M | moderate | low |
|          | H | high | moderate |

Payoff Matrix 2: Enduring Players
(Firm *T*'s Discounted Profit)

Here we see that honesty is the dominating strategy. Indeed, Firm *T* will be most prosperous if it can manage to achieve a monopoly of integrity and the reputation that brings. But in this case the forces of the market will preclude achievement of such a monopoly, because honesty will be the dominant strategy for *every* firm, and so every firm will be driven to promote the interests of society, even if that is no part of its intention.

## THE PERTINENCE OF PERFECT COMPETITION AND CONTESTABILITY

How do perfect competition and contestability enter the matter? The connection is straightforward. The relationship has two sources: the small and anonymous-firm attributes of perfect competition, and the ease of entry and exit that is a necessary attribute of both market forms and, indeed, virtually a defining characteristic of the latter.

We have seen that if the market mechanism is to enforce integrity in the quality of products and the information that their suppliers give out about the commodities they offer, the firms must be noticeable. Each firm must stand out from the crowd, so that misbehavior in terms of product quality or information about it can substantially threaten the reputation of the enterprise. A large crowd of suppliers, each of them tiny, is the contradictory of this necessary requirement of effective market enforcement of integrity in relation to product quality. Thus, the requirement of perfect competition that its firms be minuscule and homogeneous, with none displaying any features that lead customers to single them out, is by itself enough to undermine the workings of the market mechanism in this arena. An anonymous supplier who looks like every other supplier to potential customers will risk little or no loss of reputation by product degradation.

Aside from this reasoning, the costlessness and rapidity of entry and exit which have long been associated with the abstract concept of perfect competition, and which have recently received even more emphasis in connection with the equally hypothetical state of perfect contestability, are precisely the conditions that lead the repeated games of market reality to be populated by transient players. In these two market forms, because of the implied or explicit assumption that sunk costs are absent, firms lose nothing by entering a market, milking any profits it has to offer to those prepared to use fair means or foul, and then exiting in haste if and when past misconduct makes their continuing presence uncomfortable.

Such circumstances offer little comfort to suppliers who intend to exercise integrity, if widespread misrepresentation and adulteration of products lead customers to doubt the reliability of each and every supplier. If no supplier's word is believed by customers, and each product is suspected of offering minimal quality, no supplier can afford to incur the cost entailed in superior performance. The less scrupulous dealers will be able to undercut a firm that attempts to escape the ubiquitous unreliability of product quality and of the information provided about it. Costless entry and exit protect the suppliers with little conscience on these matters from any punishment by the market for their misconduct, and thereby put pressure on others with tenderer consciences to hold them in abeyance, with the threat that doing otherwise incurs the risk of financial disaster. It appears, then, that in terms of reliability of product quality and the pertinent information, perfect competition and contestability – the two "ideal" market forms we are considering here – may fall somewhat short of the perfection that their names suggest.

Yet, there may be exceptions. Even under perfect competition, where no customer can identify any particular seller, there can emerge institutional arrangements that escape the problem. A large and established institution can undertake to inspect product quality and act as guarantor to the customer. A trade association can play that role, or it can be assumed by a recognized middleman who inspects products and grades and guarantees them. It may serve the suppliers' interests to subject themselves voluntarily to such controls, for in that way they may be able to get consumers to distinguish their products from those of fly-by-night suppliers, and the costs entailed in voluntary participation in such an arrangement can be justified if they enable the participating firm to remain in business longer and to obtain higher prices for its products, whose superior quality has been recognized by purchasers.

In a contestable market, which can include very large firms, reputations can be cultivated assiduously by the individual enterprises themselves. Thus, contestability does not mean that product quality must automatically be poor or unreliable or advertising misleading. But for the firms in such a market this state of affairs is neither automatic nor easy, because the absence of sunk investments means an absence of enforced commitment to remain in the field in the long run. In Oliver Williamson's felicitous terminology, the firm is deprived of the opportunity to give hostages as guarantors of good behavior. The firm without sunk costs is deprived of the opportunity to display visible commitment to remain in the field for the long haul, and without such a commitment the value of its investment in reputation becomes correspondingly suspect. Even with the best of intentions it will be that much more difficult for the firm to convince potential customers that it is so committed. Contestability does not make the path of integrity easier.

In this light, one can perhaps consider that adopting brand names and sinking funds into their promotion are a means to escape this problem. The costs sunk in advertising the brand constitute a reduction in the market's contestability, and at the same time serve as the hostage for good behavior. This advertising is the firm's way of notifying the public that the supplier now has a good deal to lose if it is found to have adulterated its product.

Curiously, however, if brands identify the products of each and every firm, incumbent and entrant alike, then the funds (apparently) sunk in establishing brand reputation turn out not to impede contestability.[1] As in the Shapiro model, misbehavior by the incumbent firm in such circumstances causes a loss of reputation that is apt to require a long time to repair. In the interim this misstep provides an opportunity for unimpeded entry by firms determined to create a reputation for integrity, an opportunity that the miscreant incumbents will be in no position to forestall through strategic countermoves.

---

[1] This statement may appear to contradict the definition of perfect contestability as the state of affairs in which sunk costs are completely absent. But costs should not really be taken to be sunk if the period in which they can ultimately be withdrawn, however long it may be, is shorter than the time required for the incumbent to respond to entry. That is precisely why, as Sanford Grossman has noted, the availability of long-term contracts between entrants and customers can make a market contestable even if the processes of entry and exit consume considerable time.

PRELIMINARY: THE WELL-KNOWN
WASTE-PRECLUSION PROPERTY OF PERFECT
COMPETITION AND CONTESTABILITY

To understand the implications of the market forms we are considering for the role of voluntarism and social discrimination, it is necessary to recall briefly one of the best-known attributes of these market forms. This attribute is their total preclusion in the long run of all waste; that is, of all expenditures that yield no offsetting reductions in costs or contribution to revenues, and hence to profits.

The pertinent theorem is not the standard result that under a wide variety of market forms profit maximization requires the firm to produce any given output vector at minimal cost. Particularly under oligopoly, separation of ownership from management may lead the latter to pursue objectives other than profits alone, and as Williamson [1964] has emphasized, this effort may entail wasteful expenditure undertaken for management's pleasure and comfort.[2] Rather, the waste-preclusion theorem is founded on the vulnerability of the incumbent firm to loss of market to any rival that is more efficient and is consequently able to underprice the incumbent. It is the costlessness of entry and exit under perfect competition or contestability that prohibits all inefficiency, because any firm that indulges in wasteful expenditure cannot long survive the incursions of efficient entrants.

There is, of course, nothing new in this scenario. The only feature of the waste-preclusion theorem that may not be commonly recognized is the connotation of the term "waste." For, as we will see next, some outlays that are

---

[2] Of course, freedom of entry will prevent this from happening in a perfectly contestable oligopoly. But that is precisely the point. It is freedom of entry and exit, and not the profit reward for minimizing the cost of the selected output vector, which accounts for the waste-preclusion theorem.

wasteful to the impersonal and unthinking forces of the market can be regarded by the bulk of society as money exceedingly well spent, and certainly far from wasteful.

## THE WASTE-PRECLUSION THEOREM AND BUSINESS VOLUNTARISM

To put the matter bluntly, the market automatically interprets any expenditure by the firm that is undertaken only as a matter of good works as an act of unmitigated wastefulness. *Purely* charitable support of schools, hospitals, churches, or orchestras all falls into this category. The same is true of a company's decision to forgo profitable business in a country of whose government the management of the enterprise disapproves. This is necessarily so because any such decision places the firm at a competitive disadvantage relative to a rival who decides to forgo such acts. In a perfectly competitive or perfectly contestable market the firm can hope, at most, to earn zero economic profits, and can aspire even to this achievement only if its expenditures for its chosen output vector are as low as is attainable. In such a market, therefore, protracted voluntary expenditure along any of the lines indicated is a recipe for insolvency. The market then homogenizes the charitable behavior of all firms, including those with the most generous propensities and those which are most niggardly, forcing all of them alike to forgo any and all manifestations stemming from charitable instincts. Thus, in terms of the components of ethical behavior with which we are concerned in this section, no market form's performance can be rated more poorly than that of perfect competition and perfect contestability. These are market forms that infuse the spirit of Scrooge into the workings of the invisible hand.

Only one primary sort of exception is permitted, one that can be described as the exercise of enlightened self-interest.

Often, a firm contributes to charitable purposes as a matter of advertising, or to avoid having its products shunned by consumers who would otherwise disapprove of its behavior, or to make the communities in which it operates more attractive to employees, thereby improving the quality of its work force more cheaply and effectively than it can by offering them higher wages. Any such acts, if they contribute to profits, will be permitted by the invisible hand, even if they *incidentally* have charitable consequences. These are acceptable because their contribution to profits means that the market mechanism will no longer treat them as wasteful. Of course, it is common for corporate management to describe its firm's voluntary giving program as an act of enlightened self-interest of this sort. But whether or not this description is accurate in markets *generally*, in a perfectly contestable market it must be accurate because there the market mechanism rules out any giving by the firm that is not undertaken as part of the pursuit of profit.

This analysis helps to show why the voluntary performance of business in contributing to the protection of the environment has at best been mixed. Only government action which forces good behavior even upon managements that care little about such issues can permit more responsible businesspersons to undertake more than token acts toward environmental improvement in a perfectly contestable market. Making such outlays part of the necessary cost of doing business eliminates their wasteful character so far as the market mechanism is concerned. That is why a businessperson who really favors effective action to cure the environmental damage caused by the industry can contribute most effectively toward that goal *not* by attempts to institute a voluntary program within her own firm, but by supporting well-designed legislation that will impose such behavior upon the entire industry.

The same conclusion also helps to explain why professional fund raisers for nonprofit organizations, when they

approach business firms for donations, frequently empha-
size that the proposed contribution will serve the (enlightened) self-interest of the target enterprise. Not only can this
formulation help management explain the contribution to
the stockholders; it can also stem from the fund raiser's
instinctive recognition that the market mechanism offers
the company little latitude to make contributions that do
not qualify on this score.

## THE FIRM AS VEHICLE FOR MANAGEMENT'S PERSONAL CONTRIBUTIONS

One critical amendment is required to what has just been
said. There is no reason why a manager in a market that is
perfectly competitive or contestable cannot use the firm as
a conduit for his private eleemosynary contributions. If he
is eager to give money to hospitals or for protection of the
environment or some other such cause, the firm can make
the contribution for him if he is willing to accept a corresponding reduction in earnings or to offset it through harder
work or some equivalent. Perfect market equilibrium is
clearly compatible with such an arrangement, for it puts
the firm that makes the ostensible contribution at no competitive disadvantage.

Why should managers ever want to adopt such a con-
voluted means to make the contributions they desire?
The answer is that the firm can conceivably be a vehicle
offering enhanced efficiency to the donation process. It
can reduce the free-rider problem entailed in supporting
voluntaristic activities by collecting a management group
all of whose members are implicitly pledged to contribute
their shares, the commitment taking the form of accepting
employment in an enterprise offering relatively low managerial compensation and large public-service donations. It
can offer management the enhanced psychological reward

of association with a firm noted for its high moral posture. It may even be able to achieve a reputation for good conduct at bargain prices by collecting relatively small (reduced-salary) contributions from each member of the management group, if their aggregate is enough to permit a contribution by the enterprise that appears to be generous. By aggregating the contributions of management the firm may also be in a position to influence the activities of the recipients of the largess more effectively than the management of the company could do, each member of the team acting alone, with a correspondingly smaller gift. The power over the recipient conferred by the firm's centralization of the donation process may steer the beneficiary groups in directions that match the personal preferences of the management group more effectively, or it may simply serve as a means to increase the efficiency of the recipient organizations' activities, if there is truth to the view that such groups tend to be run wastefully, and that business experience can be used to infuse efficiency into the process.

However, not everything tilts the scales to favor channeling of managerial gifts through the firm. After all, giving in this way denies recognition to the donor for his charitable act that might otherwise have earned him kudos and even special privileges from the recipient organization (invitations to special festivities, better seats in the recipient nonprofit theater, and so on). Moreover, collectivized giving through the firm deprives the individual donor of control over the uses of the funds that the enterprise may funnel in directions other than that person's favorite charity.

In sum, one can imagine a sort of Tiebout model[3] [1956]

---

[3] It will be recalled that the Tiebout model describes the self-apportionment of residents among urban areas on the basis of differences among the areas in terms of quantity and quality of public services supplied and the tax rates needed to finance them. If the number of available urban areas is great, the variations in service supply and tax rate offered by

characterized by heterogeneity in the behavior of firms and in the tastes of individual executives for charitable contributions, voluntary environmental protection measures, and the like; i.e., a model in which market forces marry companies whose record of voluntarism is outstanding to the managerial personnel with a predisposition toward voluntarism and a matching willingness to sacrifice some of the compensation available to them elsewhere. How significant this combination is likely to be in practice is not clear. Casual observation suggests that the firms whose benefactions are most substantial are those which stand to gain most from the process, notably enterprises whose virtue, justly or unjustly, is felt by the public to be less than it should be, and which employ well-advertised voluntarism as a means to help improve their reputations. In any event. the sort of outlays considered in this section cannot, in the last analysis, be considered voluntary expenditures *by the firm itself.* Rather, they represent the individual contributions of the members of the management group whose voluntary acceptance of reduced compensation is the indispensable requirement for this sort of "wasteful" outlays to survive the pressures of the market under perfect competition or contestability.

## On the Market Mechanism and Social Discrimination

The connection between our focal market forms and social discrimination is identical in structure with that between the market forms and voluntarism, as just discussed. The outcomes in the two cases are, however, in a fundamental

---

them can constitute a continuum, and every resident family or firm can select that location whose offerings are best adapted to the resident's preferences.

sense, the precise opposite of each other. Perfect competition and perfect contestability prohibit virtuous business behavior in the domain of voluntarism and charitable outlays, as we have just seen. But they are equally effective in precluding social discrimination of any form, i.e., in enforcing virtue in that arena, a point explicitly recognized by Arrow [1973b, p. 10].

Paradoxically, the market's prevention of social discrimination is enforced by exactly the same machinery as its prohibition of voluntarism. In both cases, it is the waste-preclusion theorem that performs this role. If a given wage can secure for the firm the services of a woman or a Hispanic male of ability superior to that of any Caucasian male candidate for the post, then failure to hire the superior worker constitutes waste in terms of the certain response of the market mechanism. This waste is even more obvious for the firm that proposes to pay a white male more than it offers, say, to a black woman of equal or superior ability (that is, whose marginal revenue product is higher). In either case, such behavior will render the discriminating firm vulnerable to destruction through the competition of rival enterprises whose morality in terms of social discrimination is superior, or whose greed is sufficiently powerful to lead them to forgo behavior consistent with their managements' sexual or racial prejudices.

Thus, in this case, perfect competition and perfect contestability alike tolerate no business deviation from virtue. Regardless of the personal morality of a management, whether it is beyond question or reprehensible, the outcome will be exactly the same. All will be forced to knuckle under to the market's commandment: Thou shalt not discriminate (socially). Those who refuse to do so will simply find themselves ejected from the managerial ranks as their firms disappear or stockholders replace them with successors more willing to go along with the dictates of the market.

Again, as with voluntarism, there are significant exceptions. If the discriminatory bias among the members of the
firm's labor force is so strong that hiring a worker from a
minority group will impede the productivity of the enterprise, the market mechanism will permit socially discriminatory behavior, whatever the market form. Second, where
one (say) ethnic group offers *on the average* poorer performance than another (even though both include individuals whose performance prospects span the full range
of possibilities), then a high cost of search in determining
the ability of any particular job candidate can make it less
costly to discriminate systematically against the ethnic group
with the poorer average record.[4] Similarly, a management
sufficiently prejudiced to sacrifice income in order to permit the firm to engage in discrimination can also permit
such practices to persist despite competitive pressures. In
most other cases, however, the enforcement of this virtue
by perfect competition and contestability is unswerving.

SOME POSSIBLE ANTITRUST USES AND
OTHER APPLICATIONS

The preceding observations describing mandatory behavior
under two market forms imply that those patterns of
behavior are necessary conditions for one or another of the
market forms to be present.[5] That is to say, it is possible in
principle to use empirical observations of an industry's
performance in terms of social discrimination and financial
contributions to charitable institutions, broadly interpreted,

---

[4] I am indebted to Professor P. K. Pattanaik for this observation.
[5] The statement is imprecise, for it suggests that competition may be
perfect and yet the market may not be contestable. However, this is not
possible since perfect contestability is defined so as to include perfect
competition as a special case.

to test whether or not the markets are contestable or competitive. Because absence of voluntary contributions and discriminatory behavior are necessary but not sufficient conditions for prevalence of these market forms in the industry in question, such empirical observations cannot be used to demonstrate that those are the market forms which actually prevail. This type of evidence can, however, be used to prove a contention that the industry is neither perfectly competitive nor perfectly contestable, presumably implying that at least some minor degree of market power must be possessed by the firms that give contributions or practice social discrimination.

Here, several caveats require emphasis. First, no one has ever claimed seriously that *any* markets in reality are *perfectly* competitive or contestable. Both of these are, at best, useful theoretical constructs that are not to be found in reality. One can, however, possibly presume with Marshall that *natura non facit saltum* – that there is continuity in the business behavior elicited by small modifications in market structure, so that a small departure from perfection in competitiveness or contestability will permit correspondingly little social discrimination and voluntarism. By the latter, presumably, one would mean that wage differences attributable to discriminatory behavior and charitable contributions are both relatively small. The continuity premise underlying this conjecture has been disputed, however (see Schwartz and Reynolds [1983]), and it has not been tested empirically. Thus, the test of market power just suggested must be used with care; that is, with due attention to the shaky foundations of the implicit continuity premise.

The second required warning is that in such a test due account must be taken of the possibility that any voluntaristic behavior by the firm is really self-serving; i.e., that it constitutes enlightened self-interest, or that any discriminatory behavior is undertaken only to contribute to productive efficiency by promoting employee morale or to serve managerial preferences backed up by willingness to forgo a corresponding amount of compensation. For we have seen that behavior of these varieties is perfectly possible even in a regime of perfect competition or contestability. Thus, to use voluntary contributions or social discrimination as evidence that the firm in question possesses market power, one must first offer evidence that these acts did not really contribute to the profitability of the enterprise, or, at the very least, that they left profits unaffected. In light of these considerations it must be admitted that, although such a test of market power may be of theoretical interest, it probably will have little if any evaluative power in practice.

The approach offered here undoubtedly has other analytical applications. For example, by showing that the market forms under discussion deny *any* ability to sacrifice the profits of their firms to decision makers with tenderer consciences or greater hatred of underprivileged groups, it may have demonstrated also that other variations in their psychological makeup are equally denied any role by the market's forces. If so, this denial would imply that market forms may make a considerable difference in the degree of influence upon market behavior exercised by the patterns of individual economic behavior recently brought to our attention by investigators such as Tversky and Kahneman [1982] and Thaler [1980]. Though these patterns, which some behavioralists have referred to as "anomalies," may represent considerable departures from what is conventionally referred to as "rationality," it may be that where entry and exit are easy they can influence business decisions only marginally. But this is a subject that should be explored elsewhere.

Rather, I should like to end this first chapter by commenting that a "perfect" market's interdiction of voluntarism may not be as reprehensible as it may at first appear. Why, after all, should contributions to health care, education, and the arts be left to the conscience of business managements? Voluntary action leaves the dedicated business firm exposed and unprotected against the competitive advantage enjoyed by enterprises with less concerned (less ethical) managements, and surely that is not a happy state of affairs.

More than that. Why should we entrust business management, acting with other people's money, to decide which socially desirable activities merit support and to what degree? Surely, business people, whose morality (as I have several times emphasized) is not clearly superior (or clearly inferior) to that of other social groups, have no special claim on such powers. One may well argue that in the case of business support of deserving social causes, there is good reason to make the amounts and their subsequent allocation *involuntary*. That is, one may well hold that these decisions, so vital to society, should not be left to a subgroup such as company managements, but should be arrived at by the members of society as a whole, acting either individually or through their designated representatives.

REFERENCES

Akerlof, George A. "The Market for 'Lemons': Quality, Uncertainty and the Market Mechanism." *Quarterly Journal of Economics* 83 (August 1970), pp. 88–500.

Arrow, Kenneth J. [1973a] "Social Responsibility and Economic Efficiency." *Public Policy* 21 (Summer 1973), pp. 303–317.

————[1973b] "The Theory of Discrimination," in Orley Aschenfelter and Albert Rees, eds., *Discrimination in Labor Markets*. Princeton: Princeton University Press, 1973.

Heal, Geoffrey. "Do Bad Products Drive out Good?" *Quarterly Journal of Economics* 90 (August 1976), pp. 499–503.

Rashid, Salim. "Quality in Contestable Markets: A Historical

Problem?" *Quarterly Journal of Economics* 103 (February 1988), pp. 245–249.

Schwartz, M. and R. J. Reynolds. "Contestable Markets: An Uprising in the Theory of Industry Structure: Comment." *American Economic Review* 73 (June 1983), pp. 488–90.

Shapiro, Carl. "Consumer Information, Product Quality, and Seller Reputation." *The Bell Journal of Economics* 13, no. 1 (Spring 1982), pp. 20–35.

———. "Premiums for High Quality Products as Returns to Reputations." *Quarterly Journal of Economics* (November 1983), pp. 659–79.

Smith, Adam. *An Inquiry into the Nature and Causes of the Wealth of Nations, 1776*. New York: Modern Library, 1937.

Thaler, Richard. "Toward a Positive Theory of Consumer Choice." *Journal of Economic Behavior and Organization* 1 (March 1980), pp. 39–60.

Tiebout, Charles. "A Pure Theory of Locational Expenditure." *Journal of Political Economy* 64 (October 1956), pp. 416–24.

Tversky, Amos, and Daniel Kahneman. "The Framing of Decisions and the Psychology of Choice," in R. Hogarth, ed., *New Directions for Methodology of Social and Behavioral Science*, San Francisco: Jossey-Bass, 1982.

Williamson, O. E. *The Economics of Discretionary Behavior*. Englewood Cliffs, NJ: Prentice-Hall, 1964.

———. *The Economic Institutions of Capitalism*. New York: Free Press, 1985.

# 2

# "Perfect" Market Forms and Intertemporal Optimality

### William J. Baumol

## INNOVATION-CAUSED UNEMPLOYMENT: J. B. SAY AND RICARDO ON FLAWS OF THE MARKET MECHANISM

Even "perfect" markets are highly imperfect in their enforcement of business morality. That side of such market forms, which was our topic in Chapter 1, is rather infrequently discussed in the literature. At least since Keynes, another shortcoming in the performance of the quasi-ideal market forms *is* recognized universally – the involuntary unemployment that can arise in such a regime.

There is, of course, nothing surprising here. But what may be somewhat surprising is the early date at which such problems were recognized and the identity of some of the economists who devoted attention to them. Keynes, not without reason, selected David Ricardo and J. B. Say as the prime exponents of the Panglossian view that general oversupply (a "general glut") is all but impossible, and took Robert Malthus as his forbear in advocating the contrary conclusion.

But it is probably not inaccurate to say that to Keynes it was unemployment rather than overproduction that was the more pressing issue for society. At least since the appearance of the *General Theory*, the economic literature has seemed to assume that a purpose of "Say's Law" was to prove that involuntary unemployment was impossible. However, I will show here that, on the contrary, J. B. Say considered unemployment to be a very real phenomenon and a very real cause for concern. Indeed, he explicitly advocated public-works employment as a suitable means to deal with the problem. Lest this be considered yet another piece of evidence for the well-justified conclusion that J. B. Say was a highly unreliable proponent of Say's Law, at least as we understand the concept today, it will also be shown that even so uncompromising an advocate of the principle as David Ricardo was also disquieted by the possibility of unemployment, attributing it to precisely the same causes as Say.

## UNEMPLOYMENT AND THE INTRODUCTION OF MACHINERY

There is no need to review Ricardo's change of position on the effects of the introduction of machinery[1] and the controversy that followed when, in the final edition of his *Principles*, he asserted that it would adversely affect the economic position of workers, as least in the short run. It is less commonly recognized that the same point aroused the concern of J. B. Say, who concluded that new machinery

---

[1] For an exemplary discussion of the subject, see Rostow (1990), chapter 3.

might not only depress wage earnings, but that it was also likely to lead to *unemployment*. As he put it:

> Whenever a new machine, or a new and more expeditious process is substituted in the place of human labour previously in activity, part of the industrious human agents, whose service is thus ingeniously dispensed with, must needs be thrown out of employ. Whence many objections have been raised against the use of machinery, which has been often obstructed by popular violence, and sometimes by the act of authority itself.
>
> ... This ... however advantageous to the community at large, as we shall presently see, is always attended with some painful circumstances. For the distress of a capitalist, when his funds are unprofitably engaged or in a state of inactivity, is nothing to that of an industrious population deprived of the means of subsistence.
>
> Inasmuch as a machine produces that evil, it is clearly objectionable. But there are circumstances that commonly accompany its introduction, and wonderfully reduce the mischiefs, while at the same time they give full play to the benefits of the innovation. For,
>
> 1. New machines are slowly constructed, and still more slowly brought into use; so as to give time for those who are interested, to take their measures, and for the public administration to provide a remedy.
>
> 2. Machines cannot be constructed without considerable labour, which gives occupation to the hands they throw out of employ. For instance, the supply of a city with water by conduits gives increased occupation to carpenters, masons, smiths, paviours, etc. in the construction of the works, the laying down the main and branch pipes, etc. etc.
>
> 3. The condition of consumers at large, and consequently, amongst them, of the class of labourers affected by the innovation, is improved by the reduced value of the product that class was occupied upon.
>
> Besides it would be vain to attempt to avoid the transient evil, consequential upon the invention of a new machine,

by prohibiting its employment. If beneficial, it is or will be introduced somewhere or other; its products will be cheaper than those of labour conducted on the old principle; and sooner or later that cheapness will run away with the consumption and demand. Had the cotton spinners on the old principle, who destroyed the spinning jennies on their introduction into Normandy, in 1789, succeeded in their object France must have abandoned the cotton manufacture; everybody would have bought the foreign article, or used some substitute; and the spinners of Normandy, who, in the end, most of them, found employment in the new establishments, would have been yet worse off for employment ([1834] pp. 86-87, footnote omitted).

In sum, although Say believed that innovation was beneficial to society as a whole and that opposition to it was ultimately self-defeating, he was convinced that any labor-saving innovation must necessarily throw workers "out of employ" in the short run.[2] Moreover, he stressed the

---

[2] Say's discussion of machinery and its unemployment consequences much antedates Ricardo's chapter on machinery (1821). The quotations from Say just presented here also appear, virtually verbatim, in the fourth edition of the *Traité* (1819). Much of the same material already had appeared in the first edition (1803). The second edition (1814) and the third edition (1817) added Say's advocacy of public works, but in these earlier editions Say was considerably more optimistic about the transitory character of the unemployment problem. Thus, in the second and third editions the text's discussion, after mentioning the unemployment consequences of machinery, continues: "But this evil, which is always transitory, cures itself promptly. The great expansion of an output [after the rise in its productivity that caused the unemployment] reduces its price. Its cheapness expands its use; and its production, though requiring less effort, will soon enough occupy more workers than before." In the accompanying footnote, what is referred to in the fourth edition as "a benevolent administration," in the first to the third editions is "a capable administration," which "will find means to lighten this transitory and localized evil" and, besides public works, Say notes that for this purpose the government "can initially confine the use of a new machine to particular regions where labor is scarce and is demanded by other industries" (second edition, pp. 54–55, my translation).

seriousness of the problem, concluding that "the distress of
a capitalist" deprived of profitable investment opportunities ". . . is nothing to that of an industrious population
deprived of the means of subsistence."
   He went a significant step further, arguing that a virtuous government should seek to alleviate the problem and,
like a good Keynesian, proposed public works as a suitable
remedy:

> Without having recourse to local or temporary restric-
> tions on the use of new methods or machinery, which are
> invasions of the property of the inventors or fabricators, a
> benevolent administration can make provision for the em-
> ployment of supplanted or inactive labour in the construc-
> tion of works of public utility at the public expense, as of
> canals, roads, churches, or the like; in extended coloniza-
> tion; in the transfer of population from one spot to another.
> Employment is the more readily found for the hands thrown
> out of work by machinery because they are commonly al-
> ready inured to labour (p. 87, footnote).[3]

---

[3] The long run, in Say's view, is a very different matter: "So much for the
immediate effect of the introduction of machinery. The ultimate effect is
wholly in its favour. . . . The multiplication of a product commonly reduces its price, that reduction extends its consumption; and so its production, though become more rapid, nevertheless gives employment to
more hands than before. It is beyond question, that the manufacture of
cotton now occupies more hands in England, France, and Germany, than
it did before the introduction of the machinery that has abridged and
perfected this branch of manufacture in so remarkable a degree. . . . When
printing was first brought into use, a multitude of copyists were of course
immediately deprived of occupation; for it may be fairly reckoned, that
one journeyman printer does the business of two hundred copyists. We
may, therefore, conclude, that 199 out of 200 were thrown out of work.
What followed? Why, in a little time, the greater facility of reading printed
than written books, the low price to which books fell, the stimulus this
invention gave to authorship, whether devoted to amusement or instruc-
tion, the combination, in short, of all these causes, operated so effectually
as to set at work, in a very little time, more journeymen printers than
there were formerly copyists" (p. 88).

## Ricardo and Unemployment

The English classical economists who were Say's contemporaries justifiably had little confidence in Say as a reliable ally in the discussions that we describe today as "the Say's Law controversy."

With a degree of good judgment, Say raised questions about Ricardo's uncompromising position on the Law of Markets, but in the process virtually conceded that its logic hardly holds universally; i.e., he admitted, in effect, that a general glut was indeed possible. Thus, Say virtually gave away the entire position:

> Mr. Ricardo pretends that, in spite of taxes and other obstructions . . . all capitals saved are still employed, because capitalists will not lose the interest. There are, on the contrary, many savings unemployed on account of the difficulty in employing them . . . besides, Mr. Ricardo is contradicted by what happened to us in 1813, when the faults of the government ruined all commerce, and when interest of money fell so low for want of good opportunities of employing it – and by what is happening to us at this moment in which the capitals sleep at the bottom of the coffers of the capitalists (*Letters to Mr. Malthus*, p. 36, *Oeuvres Diverses*, p. 477).[4]

---

[4] At another point, Say simply claimed victory over Malthus by resorting to tautology: "our discussion on *Debouches* begins to be no more than a question of semantics. You wish me to accord the name "products" to goods that can satisfy a certain number of wants and which possess a certain value, even though that value is insufficient to repay the totality of their production costs. But the logic of my doctrine on production establishes clearly that there is no complete production unless all the inputs necessary for that piece of work are repayed by the value of the product . . . everything that is *truly produced* that cannot be sold is an outlay made thoughtlessly and without producing anything; and my doctrine on *Debouches* remains intact" (*Cours Complet*, p. 649 [my translation]. See also Malthus's comment on p. 647).

No wonder Ricardo complained to Malthus:

> I have also written some notes on M. Say's letters to you
> with which I am by no means pleased ... for the opinions
> which we hold in common, he does not give such satisfac-
> tory reasons as might I think be advanced. In fact he yields
> points to you, which may almost be considered as giving
> up the question and affording you a triumph (November
> 24, 1820, Ricardo, Sraffa [ed.], Vol. VIII, 301–302).

One could, perhaps, be led to suspect that Say's views
on unemployment were yet another manifestation of the
unreliability of his position on the Say's Law issue. Yet this
is clearly not so, or at least it is not all there is to be said
on the matter. Ricardo was surely never exceeded as an
undeviating proponent of the proposition that there can
never be a general shortfall of demand relative to supply[5]
(though Mill senior no doubt matched his zeal on this
subject). Yet Ricardo, too, granted the possibility of unemployment for limited, though perhaps substantial,
periods, and, like Say, attributed the problem to the introduction of (labor-saving) machinery.[6]

Although Ricardo's famous chapter on machinery pri-
marily emphasizes the danger that innovation can reduce
the economy's total outlay on wages, he also mentions
several times that this effect was likely to be accompanied

---

[5] It is noteworthy that, because of his consistent devotion to this sort of
position, Ricardo, the self-made man of great wealth, was constantly
accused by businessmen who were his fellow MPs of being an imprac-
tical theorist. On this subject, see Gordon (1976) pp. 55, 85, and so on.
[6] Ricardo nevertheless favored innovation for a variety of reasons. Contrary to what is usually believed about him, Ricardo was quite optimistic
on the future of the British economy, and while technological change
may not have been the primary reason for his sanguine views, it certainly
played a role. On this subject, see Gordon (1976), pp. 90–100, 131, 140,
and Rostow (1990), pp. 172–174.

by a decline in employment, as the shrinking wages fund reduced the number of gainfully employed individuals it could support. In Ricardo's words,

> I am [now] convinced that the substitution of machinery for human labour is often very injurious to the interests of the class of labourers.
>
> My mistake arose from the supposition, that whenever the net income of a society increased, its gross income would also increase; I now, however, see reason to be satisfied that the one fund, from which landlords and capitalists derive their revenue, may increase, while the other, that upon which the labouring class mainly depend, may diminish, and therefore it follows, if I am right, that the same cause which may increase the net revenue of the country *may* at the same time *render the population redundant*, and deteriorate the condition of the labourer. . . .
>
> In this case, then, although the net produce will not be diminished in value, although its power of purchasing commodities may be greatly increased, the gross produce will have fallen . . . and as the power of supporting a population, and employing labour, depends always on the gross produce of a nation, and not on its net produce, there will necessarily be a diminution in the demand for labour, population will become redundant, and the situation of the labouring classes will be that of distress and poverty.
>
> As, however, the power of saving from revenue to add to capital, must depend on the efficiency of the net revenue, to satisfy the wants of the capitalist, it could not fail to follow from the reduction in the price of commodities consequent on the introduction of machinery, that with the same wants he would have increased means of saving – increased facility of transferring revenue into capital. But with every increase of capital he would employ more labourers; and, therefore, a portion of the people thrown out of work in the first instance, would be subsequently employed; and if the increased production, in consequence of the employment of

the machine, was so great as to afford, in the shape of net produce, as great a quantity of food and necessaries as existed before in the form of gross produce, there would be the same ability to employ the whole population, and, therefore, there would not necessarily be any redundancy of people.

All I wish to prove is, that the discovery and use of machinery may be attended with a diminution of gross produce; and whenever that is the case, it will be injurious to the labouring class, as some of their number will be thrown out of employment, and population will become redundant, compared with the funds which are to employ it (Sraffa [ed.], vol. I, pp. 388–390, my italics).

## Compatibility of Unemployment with the Law of Markets?

The proponents of the "Law of Markets" apparently did not recognize that there might be an inconsistency in their espousal of that position and their conclusion that unemployment can arise (and can apparently persist for considerable periods) in the normal workings of the economy. Because, so far as I know, they never explicitly discussed the relationship between the two issues, it is entirely possible that it never occurred to them that a conflict may be involved.

In particular, it seems safe to conclude that nothing in the classical writings approximates a systematic discussion that recognizes the constraints implicit in "Walras's law" – the notion that an excess supply of labor must, by definition, have as its counterpart an excess demand for commodities or for money. It is true that Say in the second and later editions of the *Traité* does argue as part of his defense of the law of markets that people do not demand money even when they believe that this is what they are doing. Rather, his familiar counterassertion is that they want money either to buy goods for consumption or for investment ("productive consumption"). But this fairly obvious line of reasoning provides little ground on which to attribute to Say an understanding of the balance requirement of the general equilibrium (or disequilibrium).

Even more revealing is the curious position taken by Malthus on the subject and Ricardo's failure in his comments to point out the pertinence of the (Walras's law) balance requirements. One might have expected Malthus, when arguing that saving (parsimony) can lead to a general glut, to point out that this purchasing power can, indeed, constitute a demand for cash balances rather than for goods. But this is a position he explicitly rejects. "No political economist of the present day can by saving mean mere hoarding" [Sraffa, II, p. 16]. Instead, he takes a rather curious position: "It is by no means true, as a matter of fact, that commodities are always exchanged for commodities. The great mass of commodities is exchanged directly for labor, either productive or unproductive . . ." [Sraffa, II, p. 307]. He goes on to argue that, as a result, savings can lead to high wages, which will reduce profits and decrease both the incentive and the means for investment (pp. 307–309), while workers, who (in his view) have a preference for leisure ("indolence") will consequently fail to spend their high wages on goods (p. 313).

Ricardo recognizes Malthus's hopeless confusion: "But what will be the situation of the labourer? Will that be miserable?" (p. 308, see also pp. 314–315). Still, even Ricardo demonstrates no recognition of the Walras's law relationship, suggesting simply the conclusion that he, like Say, failed to recognize the problem inherent in simultaneous acceptance of the possibility of involuntary unemployment and of the law of markets.

CONTESTABILITY AND INTERTEMPORAL EFFICIENCY:
THE INCENTIVES FOR INNOVATION

Let us turn now from discussion of some of the pertinent history of economic thought to some more up-to-date materials on the relation between market forms and intertemporal efficiency.

Perfect competition or contestability also has implications for the desirability of the course taken by the innovation process. The empirical evidence does seem to suggest, with striking consistency, the character of the industry structure that is most conducive to technical advance. It is neither pure monopoly nor perfect competition that comes off with the honors. It is intermediate-sized, not giant-sized, firms that are most propitious for investment in research and development, while strong competitive pressures stimulate rapid dissemination of and widespread adoption of successful innovative steps. Contestability seems to be tailor-made to satisfy both these requirements. It certainly is consistent with largeness of firms, though not *requiring* them to be gigantic, and it brings with it effective competitive pressures, almost perfectly analogous with those associated with perfect competition while, unlike the latter, not requiring industry to be populated exclusively by midget enterprises.

This is all to the good for dynamic efficiency but, unfortunately, it is not the end of the story. Contestability does nothing to weaken the public-goods properties of knowledge production and innovation – the free-rider problem that economists seem, with good reason, to consider the most potent impediment to dynamic efficiency. The reason contestability makes no contribution here is, of course, that at bottom the problem is an externality, a warp in the price mechanism, which perfect competition also cannot correct unless means are found to eliminate the gap in the price mechanism's coverage. More than that: by entailing complete absence of barriers to entry, perfect contestability, again like perfect competition, threatens to rule out entirely the reward mechanism that elicits the Schumpeterian innovation process. That mechanism, as we know, rests on the innovator's supernormal profits, which are permitted by the temporary possession of monopoly power flowing from priority in innovation. Because *perfect* contestability rules out all market power (that is, because it permits immediate entry of imitators of any innovation), the market mechanism's main reward for innovation is destroyed by that "ideal" market form. In short, it is clearly no panacea that can claim to bring dynamic and static efficiency at the same time.

However, there is one side of the innovation process on which perfect competition or contestability may offer exemplary performance – the optimal timing of innovation, where a second-best performance can prove costly, if not fatal, to the firm.

## On the Optimal Timing of Innovation When Invention Is Continuous

Inventions almost never spring, fully developed and ready for market, from the mind of the inventor. Instead, there is almost always a protracted period of debugging and improvement, which continues even after sale of the new item has begun.

Once one recognizes the continuity of the process of invention, innovation, and imitation, the timing of the steps that make up the sequence lends itself to analysis with the aid of the standard tools of optimization. The timing of the introduction to market of a still-evolving new product illustrates the issue most clearly. Here there is an obvious trade-off between haste and deliberate delay. By rushing the introduction of the novel item in question one speeds the date at which its stream of benefits begins to flow. Two years of delay means that two years of benefits will be forgone. In addition, if speed contributes competitive strength, heading off rivals who threaten to get there first, or undermining the opportunities for profitable imitation by others seeking to invade the innovator's market, then this second cost of delay is apt to be considerable. The other side of the matter is the likelihood that delay in the date of introduction is likely to permit further improvement of the new item or further reduction in its cost. Thus, the trade-off means that some dates can be too early from the point of view of maximization of the profits from introduction of the new item, while other dates will entail excessive delay. Optimality obviously refers to the intermediate introduction date that yields maximal profits to the innovator.

The analysis that follows provides a simple model describing the analytics of the pertinent optimization process. In addition to offering the formal conditions for optimality and their economic interpretation, it provides a bit of comparative-statics analysis, showing how changes in some of the parameters, such as speeding up improvement of the process or product, or the rate of reduction of its costs, affect the optimal timing decision. The main moral that will emerge is that the timing consequences of such exogenous changes are complex, sometimes serving to delay the optimal introduction date, sometimes hastening it. This conclusion, however, will not be left entirely amorphous, for it will be possible to indicate circumstances in which the one result emerges as well as the conditions that lead to the other.

The logic of the matter can be brought out with the aid of an issue that is clearly analogous to the one that is our topic. We all know that when a consumer product's technology evolves very rapidly, the timing of the purchase poses an unnerving dilemma for the buyer. Too great a delay means deprivation of the benefits offered by the superior product, but excessive haste subjects the owner to high risk of early obsolescence. What purchaser of a personal computer, for example, has not wrestled with this decision?

This analogy also indicates the reason for the ambiguity besetting the comparative-statics results that follow. Imagine a research breakthrough that increases the speed with which the product is improved, year after year. Obviously, this will exacerbate the dilemma. Should the consumer rush out earlier, impatience with the delay having been stimulated by the enhanced rapidity with which an improved product becomes available? Or should the increased speed with which still further improvements will appear lead the buyer to hold back longer? That is, one side of the matter is the likelihood that the product will have improved to a degree that makes the opportunity cost of delay in its purchase prohibitive. On the other side, acceleration of improvement means that the rate of obsolescence of the purchase will also be increased. Let us begin to see, then, where these countervailing consequences of accelerating the improvement process are apt to leave the timing decision. For the answer we must turn to a formal model.

## MODEL: ON PURCHASE TIMING FOR A RAPIDLY IMPROVING CONSUMERS' GOOD

The simplest case, the only one that will be dealt with here, is the one in which the only effect of progress is to reduce purchase price. The product's sole purpose is assumed to be the (constant) stream of revenues that it yields. Here we use the following notation:

$R$    = the flow of revenues per unit of time, before the innovation

$S$    = the same after the appearance of the innovation (where $S > R$)

$Ce^{-wt}$ = the purchase price of the improved product at time $T$

$r$    = the (continuously compounded) rate of interest (discount)

$w$    = the rate of cost reduction through technical progress

$T$    = the purchase date

Then, the consumer's objective is to maximize

$$B = \int_{t=0}^{T} Re^{-rt} - Ce^{-(r+w)T} + \int_{t=T}^{\infty} Se^{-rt}\mathrm{d}t \qquad (2.1)$$

that is (by straightforward integration), to maximize

$$B = R/r + (S - R)/re^{rT} - Ce^{-(r+w)T}. \qquad (2.2)$$

Thus, the first-order maximum condition becomes

$$B_T = (R - S)e^{-rT} + (r + w)Ce^{-(r+w)T} = 0 \qquad (2.3)$$

where we write $B_T$ for the partial derivative of $B$ with respect to $T$. As is to be expected, equation (2.3) simply tells us that equilibrium requires the marginal opportunity cost of delay, in the form of forgone profit gain, $S - R$, to equal the associated marginal cost-reduction yield achieved through continuing improvement in technology.

To find the response of $T$, the optimal purchase date, to a change in $w$, we find the total differential of (2.3), obtaining from the requirement that equilibrium condition (2.3) must be satisfied both before and after the change in $w$

$$dB_T = B_{TT}dT + B_{Tw}dw = 0$$

or

$$dT/dw = -B_{Tw}/B_{TT}, \qquad (2.4)$$

where we know $B_{TT} < 0$ by the second-order condition. Consequently, the sign of the derivative in (2.4) will be the same as the cross-partial derivative of $B$ with respect to $T$ and $w$; that is, the numerator of (2.4). Direct differentiation of (2.3) tells us that this equals

$$B_{Tw} = Ce^{-(r+w)T}[1 - T(r + w)] \qquad (2.5)$$

which will take the sign of the expression in brackets. That is, $dT/dw$ will be positive if $T$, the (initial) optimal purchase date, is sufficiently small to yield $1 - T(r + w) > 0$, and it will be negative if $T$ is sufficiently large to reverse that sign. Let us try to find an intuitive explanation for this apparently curious result.

Here, the geometry of the matter is of some help. Figure 2.1 is a graph of $B$ [equation (2.1)], the total benefit the consumer derives from a purchase of the novel item, as a function of the date the purchase is made. The graph only suggests the asymptotic approach of the benefits curve to the horizontal axis as one moves toward the right – asymptotic behavior that is crucial for the explanation we seek. In the case shown, the selected rise in the value of the improvement rate, $w$, leads to a slight rightward move in the highest point of the curve and, hence, to an increase in the optimal value of $T$.

However, insight into the matter is offered only in Figure 2.2, which plots, as a function of $T$, the curve of *marginal* benefits of waiting (2.3); that is, it shows the behavior of $B_T$, the partial derivative of $B$ with respect to $T$. It also shows

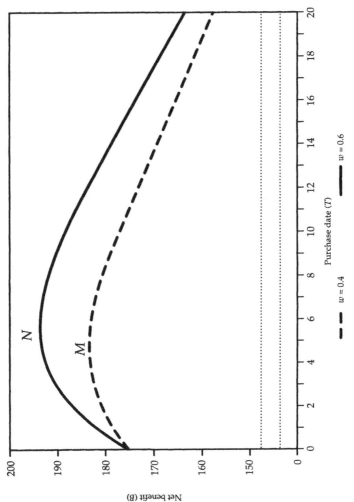

*Figure 2.1* **Net purchase benefits, As function of purchase date**

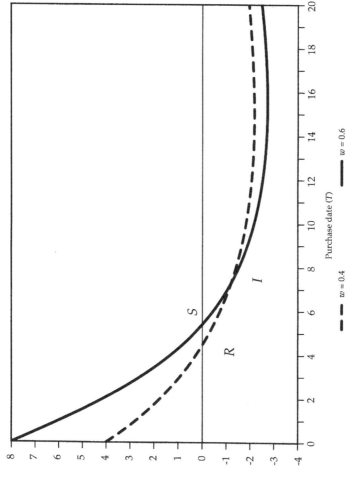

*Figure 2.2* **Derivative of net benefits, with respect to purchase date**

the effect of a change in the value of $w$ on that marginal benefits curve. We see that a rise in $w$ has two consequences. First, it raises the vertical intercept of the $B_T$ curve; that is, it adds to the initial benefits of delay – the marginal benefit of a unit addition to the elapse of time before buying, by offering the consumer a less-costly product as a reward for waiting, with the product's marginal reduction in price greater than that corresponding to a more modest value of $w$.

Second, the rise in the value of $w$ ultimately *reduces* the height of the marginal benefits curve by ensuring that the cost of the product, having approached zero sooner, must begin to level off at a lower value of $T$, meaning that relatively little more remains to be gained by further postponement of the purchase date. The initial heightening and later lowering amounts to a rotation of the curve.

The net effect of the initial raising and later lowering of the marginal benefits curve when there is a rise in $w$ is that the curve corresponding to the higher value of $w$ must at some point, $I$, intersect the marginal benefits curve for the lower $w$. Now, that means that if the optimal value of $T$, corresponding to the first-order requirement $B_T = 0$ (point $R$ or $S$) lies to the left of $I$, as in the diagram, then the rise in $w$ will increase the reward of additional waiting before buying. Thus, the optimal point, corresponding to the intersection of the $B_T$ curve with the horizontal axis, will move to the right (the move from $R$ to $S$). However, if the optimal point had been to the right of $I$, then the effect of the rise in the value of $w$ would have been the reverse, because for high values of $T$ the marginal reward of additional waiting is thereby reduced. It remains only to suggest what determines whether the optimal value of $T$ will be relatively low or relatively high. This relation can be studied directly from (2.3), which tells us that when this equilibrium condition is satisfied we must have

$$e^{wT} = C(r + w)/(S - R)$$

In other words, a rise in purchase cost, $C$, relative to the net benefits $(S - R)$ of the novel product, or a rise in the rate of reduction $(r + w)$ of the present value of that cost, must raise the optimal value of $T$ because it shifts the $B_T$ curve upward; that is, because it raises the marginal benefit of delay to some degree for every value of $T$. The intuitive reason should be obvious.

The preceding geometric discussion should suggest that our results about the consequences of a change in the rate of technological progress, as represented here by the value of $w$, do not depend on the particular functional forms we have selected for illustrative purposes, and that our conclusions, therefore, can plausibly be characterized by some degree of robustness. After all, a rise in the (percentage) rate of cost reduction will surely shift the cost curve downward, and initially cause it to fall more rapidly in the general case; but it will also cause that curve to level off earlier than before in order to avoid crossing the horizontal axis. To put it mildly, technological progress rarely, if ever, succeeds in reducing a commodity's production cost to a negative level. But these two qualitative attributes of the effect of a change of $w$ on the time derivative of cost – the initial stimulation and the later depression of the absolute rate of decline of product cost – are all that is needed for our results.

For our discussion, the pertinent point is that the delicate adjustment required for optimality in the timing process is something that market forces *can* be relied upon to handle in a regime of perfect competition or contestability, for failure to do so must constitute pure waste. Thus, this is a case in which the waste-preclusion property of these market forms *does* seem to promote the social interest.

## CONCLUDING COMMENT: ON THE PERFECTION OF COMPETITION AND CONTESTABILITY

The preceding materials were intended, fundamentally, to inject an air of reasonableness into discussions of perfect competition and perfect contestability. From earlier examinations of their efficiency properties it is clear that each of them can, in appropriate circumstances, serve as a useful instrument for promoting social welfare. But each must be used circumspectly because neither constitutes the millennium or even nirvana. They *do* have their warts and blemishes, which does not mean that they should be abandoned as tools of policy, but it does mean that these weapons must be handled with care. It is these blemishes which have been the central topic of these ruminations, with some digressions to illustrate the sort of considerations that belong on the opposite side of the balance.

REFERENCES

Gordon, Barry. *Political Economy in Parliament.* London: Macmillan, 1976.

Hollander, Samuel. *The Economics of David Ricardo.* Toronto: University of Toronto Press, 1979.

Mill, James. "Lord Lauderdale on Public Wealth." *Literary Journal* IV (July 1804), pp. 1–18.

———. Review of Say's *Traité d'Économie Politique, Literary Journal* V (April 1805), pp. 412–425.

———. *Commerce Defended.* London, 1808.

Ricardo, David. *The Works and Correspondence of David Ricardo.* P. Sraffa, ed., Cambridge: Cambridge University Press, 1951.

Rostow, W. W. *Theorists of Economic Growth: From David Hume to the Present.* New York: Oxford University Press, 1990.

Say, J. B. *Traité d'Économie Politique.* Paris, 1st ed. 1803, 2nd ed. 1814, 3rd ed. 1817, 4th ed. 1819, 5th ed. 1826.

———. *A Treatise on Political Economy,* rev. American ed., Philadelphia, 1834.

———. *Letters to Mr. Malthus,* 1820. London: G. Harding's Bookshop, 1836.

———. *Cours Complet d'Économie Politique Pratique.* Brussels: Société Typographique Belge, 1844.

———. *Oeuvres Diverses,* Paris: Guillaumin, 1848.

Stigler, George. Review of Hollander's *The Economics of David Ricardo. Journal of Economic Literature* 19 (March 1981), pp. 100–102.

Thweatt, W. D. "Baumol and James Mill on 'Say's Law of Markets.' "*Economica* 47 (November 1980), pp. 467–469.

# 3

# Social Policy: Pricing Devices to Aid the Invisible Hand

## William J. Baumol and Sue Anne Batey Blackman

Students of Adam Smith are all well aware that he recognized the imperfections of the market mechanism. Certainly he believed that the market should not be left in complete control of the allocation of resources. For example, he felt it entirely appropriate for government to supply public works that constitute no insignificant component of the nation's output. He even went so far as to argue the need for intervention in cases where there are present what we today call "externalities" (Smith [1937, p. 308]).

Yet, despite Smith's unwillingness to place his stamp of approval upon everything that the market mechanism provides, he never considered it appropriate to urge the businessperson, through appeals to conscience, to attend to the "social responsibilities" of the firm. On the contrary, he repeatedly emphasized the untrustworthiness of "merchants and manufacturers," who are always trying to escape the competitive constraints that are the instruments of the invisible hand, and so are ready to engage in a "conspiracy against the public" (p. 128). One of the basic conclusions in *The Wealth of Nations* is the unreliability of voluntarism as an instrument to secure a desirable allocation of resources. In one of its most famous passages, the author tells us that, "It is not from the benevolence of the butcher, the brewer, or the baker, that we expect our dinner, but from their regard of their own interest" (p. 14). And in the invisible-hand passage the theme is repeated, with Smith concluding, "I have never known much good done by those who affected to trade for the public good. It is an affectation, indeed, not very common among merchants and very few words need be employed in dissuading them from it" (p. 423).

Modern economists have tacitly echoed these ideas and, in at least one way, carried them a step further. The price mechanism – the instrument of the invisible hand – does, it is admitted, have some serious defects. But the remedy is not to abandon that mechanism or to superimpose other instruments with which it is not readily cross-bred. Rather, the thing to do is to use prices themselves, as far as possible, as the most promising means to cure their own shortcomings.

The father of this idea was probably A. C. Pigou, whose proposal that taxes and subsidies be used to correct the behavior of the generators of detrimental and beneficial externalities, represents precisely this sort of approach. It uses a price instrument to correct the imperfect behavior of market prices. Rather than seeking to affect the psyche of the businessperson, it seeks to change the entries in her payoff matrix in such a way that when she pursues her own goals, she unwittingly and automatically is led – by a strengthened invisible hand – to work toward those of society, or rather, of the individuals who compose it.

We begin in this chapter by offering some thoughts on the role of the socially responsible business firm in a world in which problems such as environmental deterioration are a fact of life. We then reexamine Pigou's proposal as a prime example of prices used to improve the performance of the price mechanism. We will use recent experience in environmental policy to examine its workings in practice. In particular, we focus on the U.S. Environmental Protection Agency's evolving emissions trading program, in which a very rudimentary market in pollution rights has begun to take shape. We also examine another possible variant of this approach for reharnessing the market mechanism's power to direct polluters' behavior: a proposed system of subsidies to ensure the safe disposal of toxic wastes. We provide evidence indicating that using the price mechanism to promote social goals is, in practice, not quite as straightforward or as foolproof as the theoretical models may seem to suggest. Still, they seem quite clearly to provide the most promising means to elicit socially beneficial behavior from private firms in those arenas in which the market mechanism does not do the job unaided.

## BUSINESS RESPONSIBILITY AND ECONOMIC BEHAVIOR

Under pressure from many sides, many corporate managements have been quick to assert their agreement in principle to the proposition that the firm should concern itself with the ills of society, particularly as those ills have begun to seem increasingly threatening. After all, the modern firm has shown itself to be one of the most efficient economic instruments in history. Since the beginning of the Industrial Revolution it has increased real per capita incomes perhaps twentyfold, incredible though that may seem. It has doubled and redoubled and redoubled again the energy placed at the service of humanity, and has achieved an increasing productivity of human labor that is astonishing both in its magnitude and its persistence. With such a record, what institution can be better adapted to deal with the difficult economic problems that underlie so many of our social issues?

We argue that this line of reasoning is fundamentally valid, but not if interpreted and used in the manner that generally seems to be proposed by both business and its critics. The usual proposal seems to be that industry should exhibit a massive outburst of altruism, modifying its goals to include (in addition to earning profits) improving the environment, training unskilled workers, and much more. As John Diebold put the matter: "[There is the danger that] . . . business as 'good corporate citizen' [will] start to view itself, or be viewed by others, as an all-purpose institution that should right all social wrongs. (If you added together all the rhetoric in this field you wouldn't fall far short of business being called upon to do just this!)" (Diebold [1972]).

We argue that any such undertaking may be undesirable even if it is achievable. Moreover, we give reasons why it cannot be expected to work – why the task undertaken on such a basis is likely to be managed badly. Tokenism is the natural product of such a process. Indeed, not only is business likely to prove inefficient as a voluntary healer of the ills of society, but the attempt to play such a role may well adversely affect its efficiency in the fields where it now operates and in which its abilities have been demonstrated so strikingly. We argue that the primary job of business is to make money for its stockholders. This duty does not mean that the best way to do everything is as it is done now. On the contrary, society has every reason to ask business to be much more careful in its use of the environment, to do much more to protect the interests of consumers, and so on. But we neither should nor can rely on "voluntarism" for this purpose.

If we want business to behave differently from the way it does today we must change the economic "rules of the game" so that the behavior we desire becomes *more profitable* than the activity patterns we want to modify. If pollution is made expensive enough, we will quickly be treated to a spectacular display of business efficiency in reducing emission rates. If the production of unsafe products is made sufficiently costly, one can be confident of a remarkable acceleration in the flow of innovations making for greater safety. Business will then do the things it knows how to do best and society will be the beneficiary.

Under the terms of such an approach, is there no role for "business responsibility"? Is the firm simply to pursue profits and no more? That is not quite enough. Responsibility on the part of business, from this viewpoint, has two requirements: (1) when appropriate changes in the rules are proposed by the duly constituted representatives of the community, responsible management must refrain from efforts to sabotage this undertaking; (2) business should cooperate in designing these rules to ensure their effectiveness in achieving their purpose and to make certain that their provisions interfere as little as possible with the efficient working of the economy. But, by and large, these are just the things the business world has, in effect, refused to do.

## THE DANGERS OF VOLUNTEER "SOCIAL RESPONSIBILITY"

The notion that firms should by themselves pursue the objectives of society is, in fact, a rather frightening proposition. Corporate management holds in its hands enormous financial resources. Voluntarism suggests, or rather demands, that management use these resources – other people's money – to influence the social and political course of events. But who is to determine in what way these events ought to be influenced? Who is to select these goals? If it is management itself, the power of interference with our lives and the lives of others that management is asked to assume is surely intolerable. The threat to effective democracy should be clear enough.

The point is made most clearly by recent demands that business firms exercise responsibility in their investments abroad, meaning specifically that firms should abstain from investment in countries whose governments draw the disapproval of groups that advocate such a course. A business firm may be asked to avoid or discontinue investment in countries that repress or persecute particular ethnic groups, or whose governments trample civil liberties, or are aggressive militarily, or simply oppose United States foreign policy with sufficient vigor. We do not want to argue here either the efficacy or the desirability of boycotts. Nor do we wish to defend the countries that have been attacked by critics of corporate policies on overseas investment. We, too, are repelled by some of their governments. In sum, we are not arguing for isolation or for ignoring repression. Rather, we question the notion that American business should attempt to arrogate to itself the determination of our foreign policy.

It may or may not make sense to boycott some foreign government. But we do not want a business management to decide which government should be boycotted. And certainly we do not want management to use the capital we have entrusted to it to impose its notions of international morality upon the world. One can be equally suspicious of the proposal that the business executive be empowered to decide on the allocation of other people's money under their control among the competing claims of hospitals, educational institutions, arts organizations, and environmental causes. Why should the businessperson be entrusted with the power to set such priorities for all of society?

Again, in Diebold's words:

> I personally believe [the choice of social goals] is the job of the politician working in a democratic political process. The businessman as businessman should not be making essentially social decisions. The businessman should be the tool who responds to market demand by making what society shows it wants. Do not make him more mighty than that.

An increase in corporate power is probably the last thing that those who call for greater "corporate responsibility" would want. Yet that, paradoxically, is precisely where some of their prescriptions lead.

## THE TOKEN ACTIVITIES OF BUSINESS

Predictably, a considerable gap has separated business's glowing accounts of its own accomplishments from its actual achievements. Newspapers report many cases in which their public-relations agents have run far ahead of what companies have actually accomplished. A recent example is the growing number of manufacturers attempting to make themselves seem "environment friendly" (and thus appeal to the "green market") by labeling their products recyclable, when there is no actual recycling of the products. Such claims have elicited action from states attorneys-general and other government agencies charging false advertising and have resulted in a number of industries dropping their claims.[1] The conclusion to be drawn here is *not* that businesspersons are particularly dishonest. The honesty and the degree of concern with social issues will

---

[1] John Holusha, *The New York Times*, January 8, 1991, pp. D1 and D5. Copyright © 1991 by The New York Times Company. Reprinted by permission.

vary from one businessperson to another, as it does elsewhere.[2] But even with the best intentions, given the economic rules of the game as they exist today, the individual businessperson cannot reasonably be expected voluntarily to pursue society's environmental goals.

It is the prime virtue of the competitive process that it leaves little up to the good will of individual managements. A business firm which is inefficient or which does not provide the public with the products it wants is given short shrift by the market mechanism. It is a merciless process that has no pity for the weak, ineffectual firm. But that same competitive process which prevents laziness or incompetence also precludes voluntarism on any significant scale. The business executive who chooses voluntarily to spend until it hurts on the environment, on training the handicapped, or on support of higher education is likely to find that he is vulnerable to undercutting by firms without a social conscience that, by avoiding such outlays, can supply outputs more cheaply. The invisible hand does not work by inducing business firms to pursue the goals of society as a matter of conscience and good will. Rather, when the rules are designed properly it gives management no other option.

## USING THE PRICE MECHANISM TO PURSUE SOCIAL GOALS

Economists have long argued that when faced with mounting social problems one should not abandon the profit

---

[2] Consumers' records of voluntary compliance in these areas are no better than those of business firms. It is easy to document cases in which there has been a response that is less than spectacular to voluntary programs for recycling solid wastes, for increased use of carpools, or for installing inexpensive emission-control kits in automobiles.

system or undermine its workings. Rather, if one is really serious about the social goals that are being urged upon business, one should use that powerful economic instrument, the price mechanism, to help attain them. For example, it has been suggested that the reason industry (like others) has been so free in using the atmosphere as a dumping ground for its pollutants is that clean air is a valuable resource available for use by anyone at a price far below its cost to society. Imagine what would happen if, say, coal or cloth or some other such resource were supplied free to anyone who wanted to use it, in any desired quantity and with no accounting for its manner of utilization. The resulting wastes and inefficiencies are all too easy to envision. But that is precisely what is encouraged when society, by long tradition, makes available on precisely those terms the use of its water, its air, and its other resources that are held in common.

Economists have therefore suggested that an appropriate remedial measure is to levy an adequate charge for the use of such resources. If made costly enough, their use will rapidly become more sparing and less inefficient. There are many virtues in such a program. Any such system of charges (for example, a tax of $x$ dollars per gallon on the discharge of certain types of effluents into waterways) is as automatic as any tax-collection process. It does not involve the uncertainties of detection of violations and of the subsequent judicial process. It does not rely on the vigor of enforcement agencies, which seems so often to wane rapidly. It offers its largest rewards in the form of decreased taxes to the firms that are most efficient in reducing emissions. It thereby makes use of the full force of the market mechanism as an instrument of efficiency. And these are not all the virtues that can be claimed for such an arrangement. From the point of view of the businessperson, too, a great deal can be said for it.

First, such a pollution charge is a natural extension of the profit system, which business should welcome as a means to strengthen its workings and its social responsibility in the long run. Second, this arrangement protects business from the notion that it is engaged in criminal activity when in the course of ordinary productive operations wastes are unavoidably generated. By making business pay the full social costs of its activities, including all the resources used in its operations, we recognize clearly that business is engaged in a normal and commendable productive process, rather than the antisocial activity of which it is all too easily suspected under current arrangements. Third, such a set of rules protects the firm against undercutting by competitors when it does behave in a manner consistent with social objectives – no room is created for undercutting when everyone is subject to similar costs imposed for the protection of society.[3] Finally, and this should in the long run be most important of all to the businessperson, the proposal avoids the imposition of direct controls by the government. A management is not told how to run its business – whether to install taller smokestacks or to recycle or to adopt a higher-grade fuel. Rather, emissions are made highly unprofitable and the businessperson is invited to decide for herself the most effective ways of reducing them or of eliminating them altogether. There need be no accelerated erosion of the freedom of enterprise. Changing prices of inputs are a normal business phenomenon. Fuel can be expected to grow more expensive as its scarcity increases, and other inputs grow cheaper as innovation improves their productive technology, but neither of these changes

---

[3] Of course, if such a rule applies only in a small geographic area, it does not protect the firm from the competition of suppliers located elsewhere. But this reservation argues that such rules should cover as large a geographic area as possible, not that they should be avoided.

*Social Policy*

weakens the prerogatives of management. Similarly, the imposition of a pollution charge corresponding to the social costs of the use of environmental resources does not interfere with the managerial decision process. It merely changes the structure of the economy's rewards to the company, increasing the profitability of the behavior desired by the community.

## Changing the Economic "Rules of the Game"

This proposal is not, in itself, our major point here. Rather, it illustrates what we mean by a change in the rules of the game. Many other types of changes in rules are possible. The type most frequently talked about is direct controls: for example, quotas assigned to firms or to municipal sewage treatment plants, specifying maximum quantities of pollution emissions and standards of purity that they must meet before they can be discharged into waterways. All sorts of things can be specified by direct controls. They can require the installation of specified types of devices that limit the emissions of automobiles; they can make mandatory the use of various safety devices. The range and variety of such regulations should be obvious enough.

Besides such direct controls, whose enforcement is left to government agencies, other changes in rules are also possible. Legislation authorizing legal suits by interested private citizens has often been advocated. Something intermediate between direct controls and the fiscal methods described above is represented by the construction of treatment facilities by governmental agencies, whose costs polluters are then required to bear.

The essential point is that all these procedures involve changes in the rules themselves. The firm is not expected to do anything as a pure act of benevolence. Rather, it is faced with a new set of conditions under which it and its competitors must operate, and they must adapt themselves as effectively as they can. The two most important characteristics of such changes in the rules, for us, are that there is nothing voluntary about them, and that they apply equally to all competitors. In this way management is freed from pressures to undertake a role in the policy-making process which it has no reason to want and which society has every reason to fear. Moreover, the firm is protected from attacks by those who stand ready to undercut it at the first opportunity, an opportunity that would be opened were the firm to bow to social pressures for voluntarily pursuing its social responsibilities.

## The Response of Business

With such potential advantages to the firm, to the free-enterprise system, and to society, one might have expected that at least a substantial segment of the business community would have welcomed with open arms such changes in the rules. After all, does not that change constitute a true acceptance by business of its social responsibility, through an arrangement that elicits desirable behavior from everyone and avoids the ineffectiveness and inequities of voluntarism?

But little of the sort has in fact occurred. Let us illustrate. When we first undertook to prepare a much earlier version of this paper, it seemed appropriate to see what might be suggested by the newspapers. For twelve days we searched *The New York Times* for relevant materials and encountered not a single example of industry support for anything that could be interpreted as a change in the rules designed to strengthen the protection of the public's interests. But we *did* find a profusion of pertinent cases in which industry took the opposite position, as summarized in the following excerpts.[4]

> *Example 1: Consumer Protection*
> "Legislation to create a consumer protection agency which would represent consumers before federal courts and regulatory agencies died on the Senate floor, a victim of a filibuster. The bill, regarded as the most important consumer measure of the present Congress, commanded majority support in the Senate; but it ran into intensive opposition from industry."[5]

> *Example 2: Regulation of Phosphate Utilization*
> "Administration officials reported today that Governor Cahill will push next month for final legislative approval of a controversial measure that would give New Jersey the power to ban phosphates from detergents and other cleaning agents. . . . State officials reported that the Senate's Republican leadership now favors the measure, which died last year in committee at the hands of the detergent industry and organized labor interests in the Legislature."[6]

> *Example 3: Control of Strip-Mining*
> "Legislation to provide for regulation of the strip-mining of coal and the conservation and reclamation of strip-mining areas was passed by the House today and sent to the Senate. The Vote was 265 to 75.

---

[4] We do not mean to suggest that this is a random sample; i.e., that this represents the number of such stories one would encounter in a representative two weeks. The period that happened to be chosen encompassed the adjournment of Congress and so the number of pieces of legislation whose fate was settled was unusually high.

[5] J. W. Finney, *The New York Times*, October 8, 1972, Section 4, p. 1. Copyright © 1972 by The New York Times Company. Reprinted by permission.

[6] R. Sullivan, *The New York Times*, October 11, 1972, p. 1. Copyright © 1972 by The New York Times Company. Reprinted by permission.

"The House measure would give the Interior Department authority to issue cease-and-desist orders against any surface-mining of coal when the health and safety of the public or employees is involved; to designate certain areas as unsuitable for strip-mining if lasting injury would be caused to the environment; and to issue and revoke permits for strip-mining.

"Six months after enactment, no coal strip-mining could be conducted without a permit. Except for reclamation plans, any permit application would have to have the written consent of the owner of the surface of the land.

Carl E. Bagge, president of the National Coal Association, representing coal operators, said the bill was a punitive, unrealistic measure which would reduce the nation's production of coal by 25 percent almost overnight.

Mr. Bagge assailed the bill as an "arbitrary, simplistic solution" to a complex problem. He urged the Senate to reject it, contending that it was too late in the session to amend the House bill to one that was satisfactory."[7]

*Example 4: Safety of Drug Products*
"In an effort to persuade the House to narrow the legal remedies in a pending product safety bill, Thomas G. Corcoran, a Washington lawyer who represents major drug interests, pointed out that the bill could overburden the Federal courts with new cases. The drug industry was leading the fight against the bill, which is now nearing enactment."[8]

*Example 5: Inspection for Disease-Carrying Pets*
"When the polyethylene bag was invented, the tropical fish industry ballooned. Its bubble may burst, pet supply wholesalers say, because of a proposed Federal law affecting fish imports, modeled after other regulations restricting

---

[7] *The New York Times*, October 12, 1972, p. 1. Copyright © 1972 by the New York Times Company. Reprinted by permission.
[8] F. P. Graham, *The New York Times*, October 14, 1972, p. 1. Copyright © 1972 by the New York Times Company. Reprinted by permission.

the sale of turtles and banning the import of certain birds to prevent communicable disease.

'We recognize the need for inspection and regulation,' says Richard Kyllo of Saddle River, vice president of the newly organized Tropical Fish Institute of America. 'But the new codes were enacted in a state of panic. They are so loosely worded that they leave an open road to any kind of interpretation.'

New Jersey is among many states that recently passed restrictions on selling turtles unless they were found free of salmonella, a bacteria that causes intestinal disease. The regulations were a reaction to the death in 1969 of a 9-year-old turtle owner in Connecticut."[9]

*Example 6: Information on Restaurant Sanitation*
"The New Jersey Public Health Council tonight ordered all restaurants in the state to post the results of their state sanitary inspection reports conspicuously near their entrance, in an effort to open heretofore confidential inspection files to public scrutiny. 'We have kept intact our promise to provide consumer health protection unequaled anywhere in the country,' Dr. Cowan said.

As a result, the restaurant industry, which bitterly opposed the open posting of inspection reports at a public hearing here last month, is expected to contest the council's order in the courts."[10]

*Example 7: Water-Pollution Control*
"The Senate and House of Representatives overrode today President Nixon's veto of the Federal Water Pollution Control Act of 1972, which thus becomes law and authorizes $24.6 billion over three years to clean up the nation's lakes and rivers. During nearly two years of Congressional deliberation on the bill, the White House had supported industry's

---

[9] J. Marks, *The New York Times*, October 15, 1972, p. 96. Copyright © 1972 by the New York Times Company. Reprinted by permission.
[10] R. Sullivan, *The New York Times*, October 17, 1972, p. 1. Copyright © 1972 by the New York Times Company. Reprinted by permission.

opposition to many of its provisions, particularly the goal of no discharges of industrial pollutants by 1985 and the setting of limitations on effluents for classes of industry."[11]

And, more recently:

*Example 8: Pollution Controls for Gasoline-Powered Garden Equipment*
"In an action that is believed to be the first effort ever to regulate exhaust from [gasoline-powered lawn mowers, leaf blowers, hedge trimmers, snow blowers] . . . and other 'utility' machines, [California's] . . . powerful Air Resources Board is expected to order manufacturers . . . to reduce pollutant emissions by 55 percent in two steps starting in 1994. . . . But industry leaders maintain that the rules are more likely to double the retail prices of such products by 1994 and to shut them out of the California market altogether by 1999, when the second tier of rules take effect. . . . [The] president of the Portable Power Equipment Manufacturers Association . . . [said], 'the 1999 rule puts our industry out of business in California.'"[12]

Other illustrations are easy enough to provide. The billboard industry, the manufacturers of plastics, of tetraethyl lead, and many others have all played the same game. The outcries have become familiar: proposed regulations are "punitive," "unworkable," "staggeringly expensive," and even "ruinous." But we rarely hear of industry representatives who volunteer drafts of alternative regulations that really prove to be effective. Certainly we have never heard of an industry representative arguing that a proposed piece of legislation is not sufficiently strong!

Yet firms *have* responded in some degree to the public

[11] E. W. Kenworthy, *The New York Times*, October 18, 1972, p. 26. Copyright © 1972 by the New York Times Company. Reprinted by permission.
[12] Robert Reinhold, "California Acts on Pollution in the Garden," *The New York Times*, December 14, 1990, pp. A1 and A29. Copyright © 1972/90 by The New York Times Company. Reprinted by permission.

pressure and growing awareness of the issues. As one knowledgeable observer reports,

> The environmental ethic . . . has had an unmistakable effect on corporate decision makers. In part this has been a matter of necessity. Virtually every corporate decision – whether concerning the construction of a new plant, the modernization or closure of an existing one, the introduction of a new product line, or the modification of a current product – requires a careful analysis of the regulatory implications. But the heightened sensitivity regarding the environment is not altogether forced, as a recent example indicates.
>
> In the 1986 amendments to the Superfund law, Congress tacked on a separate statute, the Emergency Planning and Community Right-to-Know Act of 1986. Among other things, this law required that for the first time certain classes of manufacturing facilities report annually their emissions of a large number of toxic chemicals into the air, water, and land, even if these emissions were routine and allowable under all other environmental statutes. The statute was designed primarily to make information available to state and local officials, community groups, and individual citizens. When in mid-1988 the chairman of the board of the Monsanto Company saw the volume of emissions his company reported, he immediately pledged to reduce those emissions by 90 percent over the next five years. He did this in spite of the fact that Monsanto was violating no laws with those emissions and that such an ambitious cutback would be quite expensive, expressing the view that Monsanto could and should do better – and would. While one should not read too much into such decisions, they are not altogether uncommon, and they reflect an enhanced sense of environmental responsibility on the part of many large corporations. This, too, is a very real accomplishment of the last two decades of environmental legislation and regulation (Portney [1990, p. 280]).

## FISCAL INCENTIVES FOR ENVIRONMENTAL POLICY: SOME RECENT EXPERIENCE

Having reviewed the arguments supporting the use of fiscal incentives as effective means to protect the environment, we turn to another side of the story: the evidence that the use of these instruments is not quite as straightforward as is sometimes imagined. Taxes upon polluters or marketable pollution permits both raise issues of distributive equity and political palatability, which have often been noted. But the problems go well beyond this.

One of the main arguments of those who advocate, for example, effluent charges over a system of direct controls is the contention that the former benefit from the certainty of death and taxes – that taxes are often collected more or less routinely and automatically – whereas direct controls depend upon the vigilance of the regulatory agency, its ability to catch the polluter who violates the rules, to gather the evidence needed to convict him, to carry the process of prosecution through successfully, and, finally, to get the courts to impose more than token penalties. Unfortunately, this contrast is an oversimplification. Knowledgeable and sympathetic lawyers assure us that any effluent-charges legislation passed by Congress is certain to be tied up in the courts for years. Those who are likely to suffer the financial burden of pollution charges can be relied upon to seek relief by every available avenue. And the law provides grounds enough for the purpose. If, for example, the courts do follow Pigou in interpreting effluent charges as *taxes*, it is very likely that they will not permit a regulatory agency to play any role in setting the fees, for that would usurp a legislative prerogative. More important, they would very likely reject geographic differences in the levels of these charges based on differences in damage done by equal emissions in different areas, for any such differences in tax rates, either from one state to another, or within different areas of any one state, are likely to be considered discriminatory.

These barriers to effective use of effluent charges may be considered artificial – the product of defective human institutions. But other problems arise directly out of the nature of the issue. Having been involved in the months of effort required to draw up a draft statute, we are painfully aware of the extent to which the task is impeded by our imperfect knowledge and analysis. Water is polluted by a vast number of impurities. How many of them should be subjected to its individual effluent charge? What relative rates should be set for the different pollutants, particularly for those *suspected* of constituting serious threats to health, but for which the evidence is not reasonably conclusive (and, indeed, may never be)? What does one do about emissions of agencies of federal, state, and local governments, which sometimes spew forth the bulk of our waterways' pollutants?

Perhaps more serious still are the problems of continuous source monitoring. Some types of direct controls share with effluent charges the need for reliable information on the quantities of the different emissions of the individual polluter. After all, we can neither send the polluter his monthly effluent-charges bill nor can we apprehend him for violating an emissions quota if we do not know how much he is spewing forth. However, it must be emphasized that this is *not* true of all methods of direct control. A law that requires installation of smokestack scrubbers or retrofitting aircraft with noise-abatement equipment might be monitored well enough by occasional checking of the equipment to verify that it is installed and in operating condition. Though this sort of control is anathema to most economists, it is clear that it does escape the need for metering.

This point is important because metering of most pollutants is still an extremely costly, time-consuming, and primitive affair. Indeed, much of today's monitoring technology is not even designed for the continuous daily measurement of emissions. Instead, the equipment is developed susually as a means to determine whether a polluter has installed equipment capable of producing an acceptable level of emissions; i.e., whether the polluter is initially in compliance with pollution regulations. One recent assessment of monitoring technology describes the dilemma:

> The source [of pollution] is required to run its production equipment at particular levels and to demonstrate that its pollution control equipment can produce acceptable discharges – discharges consistent with its permit . . . the test does not involve actual operations. . . . And there is certainly no need for speed in setting up the measurement equipment. In this setting, complex and awkward measurement technology could be tolerated in the interests of keeping measurement errors low. The same is not true when continuing compliance is to be monitored. In that context, ease with which equipment can be transported, brevity of set-up time, and economy of operation are more important . . . (Portney et al. [1990, p. 268]).

Even the monitoring of noise pollution, for which the equipment is quick, accurate, and sophisticated, suffers from a crucial shortcoming. Unless the noise is produced by a single, well-identified source, this equipment cannot apportion the responsibility for noise among those who generate it. Highways represent the extreme example. Their sounds can be a source of extreme annoyance, but the generators of the sounds are very large in number and extremely mobile, so that it is virtually impossible to track down the screeching motorcycle that passed at 2:00 A.M., or the loud truck that woke people again a half hour later. Construction of reflecting sound barriers, and prohibition of particularly noisy retread truck tires, inefficient though they may be, have so far proved more effective means for dealing with the matter.

None of this discussion is intended to constitute an appeal to economists to retreat from their predilections for pricing instruments as the ideal means to strengthen the invisible hand. Rather, it is intended to point out to them at least the outer layer of complexities that can beset the approach, that they may be better prepared to deal with the resulting difficulties. It also is an appeal for further research on the means needed to make the approach work – research on metering techniques, research on practical criteria on which to base reasonable relative prices for different pollutants, research on the pertinent legal issues, and so on. This is one case in which the call for further research is not just a conventional platitude put forth to conceal the absence of substantial ideas. Here we *do* have a very good idea of what information we lack and, therefore, the problems effectively prescribe the sort of research that is required. As we will see next, however, not all environmental market measures give rise to such formidable obstacles.

### TOWARD OPERATIONAL FISCAL INCENTIVES

One remedy for pollution, long advocated by economists as an alternative to direct controls, is the issue of a limited number of pollution *permits* to be sold on a free market. About fifteen years ago, the U.S. Environmental Protection Agency, motivated by numerous theoretical studies suggesting huge potential savings in pollution-control costs and under pressure from approaching deadlines for air-pollution standards, began to experiment with a program of emissions trading. The four components of this program

– netting, offsets, bubbles, and banking – work together as a very rough approximation to a market in emissions permits.

*Netting* was introduced in 1974. This program allows a company to create a new source of air pollution in one of its factories if it simultaneously cuts emissions from another source within the same factory, thus effecting an internal trade of emissions. The next program introduced by the EPA was *offsets*, which allow *new* factories or other new sources of air pollution to be constructed in areas where pollution standards have not been met, so long as their emissions are more than offset by reductions in pollution from elsewhere; i.e., this program permits external trades between different companies. For example, firm A can open for business if it can induce firm B to adopt pollution controls that cut down B's emissions by an amount at least equal to A's proposed emissions.

So far, few offset transactions have worked out in quite this way. Instead, under this program most firms have obtained permits to build new plants by internal offsets, that is, by offsetting reductions in pollution from other plants they own, and in some cases by offsetting reductions in emissions by some government agency. For example, state officials in Pennsylvania switched to nonpolluting road-paving materials on the state's highways to offset the pollution from a new Volkswagen auto-assembly plant in New Stanton.

The *bubble* program, begun in 1979, is similar to the offsets program but applies to firms already in operation rather than to newly established plants or firms. With the old direct controls, each pollution discharge point in a factory or plant was regulated. But under the bubble concept, all operations of the firm are considered to be encased in an imaginary bubble with a single discharge point; the firm is permitted to satisfy the air pollution ceiling for its "bubble" in any way it finds most economical. The EPA does not care what goes on inside the bubble; that is, whether emissions come from one point or another, as long as emissions from the entire bubble stay within the required limits.

*Banking*, the last element in EPA's emissions-trading program, permits firms whose total emissions fall below the required limits to sell the unused emission rights to other firms whose "bubbles" are not performing so well, or to store these extra rights in an emission-reduction "bank" for future use or trade.

The level of activity within each of these programs has varied widely, with netting the best-received element – accounting for between 5,000 and 12,000 transactions through the mid-1980s. About 2,000 offset trades have taken place, although only 10 percent of them have been the external trades that most closely mimic the ideal market-place in pollution permits. Fewer than 150 "bubbles" have been approved, and there has been almost no banking thus far. Nevertheless, one expert concluded that the emissions-trading program has "clearly afforded many firms flexibility in meeting emission limits, and this flexibility has resulted in significant aggregate cost savings – in the billions of dollars."[13]

Another environmental issue, the problem of disposing of toxic wastes, has proved to be particularly intractable.

---

[13] Hahn [1989, p. 101]. The new Clean Air Act, signed into law late in 1990, makes use of market-based incentives to an even greater degree than its predecessor. For example, the provisions dealing with sulfur-dioxide pollution from electric utilities grant the utilities tradable rights to emit a specified number of tons of $SO_2$ per year. Utilities that pollute less than their specified rights are free to sell them (to other utilities or even to environmental groups that could then "retire" them) or bank them for future use. The program promises potentially huge cost savings – $2 to 3 billion, according to Robert Hahn (Carpenter [1990]).

And yet, it too may be controllable by fiscal means, though of a type rather different from those suggested by Pigou.[14] The technical and economic magnitude of the problem of disposal of toxic wastes has not yet been reliably estimated. It may, however, prove more serious for human health than all other environmental problems combined. And yet we have made virtually no progress toward its resolution. Official policy in this area can be characterized as the "gangbuster" approach, under which the bad guys who pollute are apprehended by the police who see to it that justice is done. We have ignored the lesson of Prohibition, which tells us that this approach is doomed to failure. Its chief function is to create a protected market with high profits for the professional criminals who do not hesitate to dump hazardous wastes illegally and in ways that increase the danger to the public substantially. This direct-control approach also suffers from a perpetual lack of funds for effective enforcement. States and municipalities are able to pursue only the most blatant offenders, while most illegal dumping of toxic wastes goes unpunished.[15]

But there does seem to be an approach that has a chance of dealing with the problem effectively, much as it goes against our idea of how the world *should* operate: make it *financially advantageous* to dispose of wastes properly. This result can be achieved by a system of subsidies for proper and safe disposal of toxic wastes. Inspection and coercion are useless because no one knows who produces these wastes or who is currently holding them. Only a financial

---

[14] The following material is extracted from a *New York Times* article written by W. J. Baumol and E. S. Mills [1985]. We are grateful to Professor Mills and the *Times* for permission to use the material. Copyright © 1985 by The New York Times Company. Reprinted by permission.

[15] See Michael Winerip, *The New York Times*, January 8, 1991, p. B1. Copyright © 1991 by The New York Times Company. Reprinted by permission.

incentive that succeeds in inducing these persons to comply voluntarily may have a chance of working, and may well prove far less expensive than cleaning up the damage caused by indiscriminate dumping.

Although for more than half a century economists have advocated fees for pollution discharges or the sale of marketable permits, few have proposed such government incentive programs for the disposal of toxic wastes. The reasons for their hesitancy to endorse such a program are the very reasons that make the problem so serious: the inability of government agencies to measure or estimate harmful discharges with tolerable accuracy and at tolerable cost. Pinpointing organic discharges from, say, a sewage treatment plant or sulfurous discharges from a thermal electric plant is relatively simple. The quantities of discharges can be metered or estimated on the basis of the flow of materials into the facility, and suitable charges can then be levied on the basis of that information. The problem of toxic wastes is different. Tens of thousands of chemical compounds are produced in the United States, and some 6,000 new compounds are discovered each year. After years of expensive federal toxic-waste control programs, we do not have a list of chemicals that are likely to be harmful even in small quantities, nor is there any prospect that such a list can be compiled. Certainly hundreds of these chemicals, not to mention radioactive wastes and other pollutants, are harmful to people, animals, water, and crops even in tiny doses. Yet the flow of wastes continues to pour out of thousands of manufacturing companies, large and small, hospitals, laboratories, and probably many other sources. Many are small facilities whose products and functions change rapidly. Too many find illegal disposal to be cheap and easy, and arrange to have harmful quantities of these substances dumped into sewers, drains, streams, or on the roadside from a tank truck whose spigot is left open on a rainy night.

The government's response to this growing peril has been to adopt increasingly severe programs to enforce a roomful of regulations – "cradle-to-grave" recordkeeping, controls on production, transportation, storage and use, complex evidence gathering and commando like raids on suspect sites. Such actions make for dramatic headlines, litigation, and confrontation, but there is no reason to believe that they have made or will make significant progress in protecting the nation's health. Enforcement is too sporadic and evasion too easy to make a significant dent in the problem. One would expect, however, that such measures would hasten the criminalization of the disposal industry.

Economic incentives seem the only viable option. The main reason for illegal disposal is that it is cheaper than compliance with the law, and it is in the public interest to reverse the order of these costs. Although no way has been found to impose charges on harmful disposal, we can subsidize safe disposal. All that is needed is for governments in each state to identify a set of acceptable disposal facilities and pay for delivery of toxic wastes at the sites. The subsidy could be financed out of a general tax on the industries concerned, so as to constitute neither gain nor loss to these industries.

A small set of disposal procedures can work for a large variety of highly toxic chemicals. High-temperature incineration is acceptable for many, hardened burial for some, and reprocessing for others. Promising techniques for efficient disposal are available and research can provide us with others. Determining the magnitude of the subsidy for toxic substances delivered to the site will not be easy. If the subsidy is too low it will fail to attract wastes into channels for proper disposal and chemicals will continue to be dumped on the highways. If the subsidy is too high, excessive amounts will be produced, probably deliberately, because money can be made merely by delivering the wastes to the authorities and collecting the subsidy. Thus, proper setting of the subsidy probably will require careful monitoring and periodic adjustment.

Subsidizing toxic-waste disposal is, inherently, an idea that is bound to be unattractive to all. It is hard to countenance the idea of paying people to do what they should be doing anyway. But one thing is certain: the right subsidy would dramatically alter discharge patterns. If there is even a small probability that the problem of toxic-waste disposal will prove to be as serious as we are told it is, the money will be well spent.

### CONCLUDING COMMENTS

We remain confirmed supporters of pricing devices as a means to strengthen the invisible hand, and we continue to suspect the effectiveness of business voluntarism dedicated to meeting social responsibilities. The catalogue of shortcomings of direct controls and other standard instruments of regulation is long and impressive. But economists must nevertheless remember that the ideal pricing mechanisms that populate our theoretical models must undergo modification as they encounter new difficulties when they enter the world of reality. By preparing ourselves for the resulting problems, economists can become more effective advocates of the pricing approaches. More important, they can make themselves more useful in the demanding task of translating the theoretical concepts into usable and acceptable measures for practical policy.

### REFERENCES

Baumol, William J., and Edwin S. Mills. "Paying Companies to Obey the Law." *The New York Times.* Forum, October 27, 1985, p. F3.

Carpenter, Betsy. "A Marketplace for Pollution Rights." *U.S. News and World Report*, November 12, 1990, p. 79.

Diebold, John. "The Social Responsibility of Business," address at the conference on "An Economic Society for Man," June 21, 1972.

Hahn, Robert W. "Economic Prescriptions for Environmental Problems: How the Patient Followed the Doctor's Orders." *Journal of Economic Perspectives* 3, no. 2 (Spring 1989), pp. 95–114.

Portney, Paul R. "Overall Assessment and Future Directions," Chapter 8 in Paul R. Portney, ed., Roger C. Dower, A. Myrick Freeman III, Clifford S. Russell, and Michael Shapiro, *Public Policies for Environmental Protection*. Washington, D.C.: Resources for the Future, 1990.

Smith, Adam. *An Inquiry into the Nature and Causes of the Wealth of Nations*, Edwin Cannan, ed. New York: Modern Library, 1937 (reprint of 5th ed. dated 1789).

# WILLIAM J. BAUMOL
# PUBLICATIONS

1991

**Books**

With Alan S. Blinder. *Economics: Principles and Policy*, 5th ed. San Diego: Harcourt Brace Jovanovich, 1991, 892 pp.

**Chapters in Books**

"Wages, Virtue and Value: What Marx Really Said." Chapter 2 in G. A. Caravale, ed., *Marx and Modern Economic Analysis*, vol. I: Values, Prices and Exploitation. London: Edward Elgar, 1991, pp. 45–70.

"Comment on 'Expectation and Plan: The Microeconomics of the Stockholm School,' by Claes-Henric Siven," and "On Formal Dynamics: From Lundberg to Chaos Analysis," in Lars Jonung, *The Stockholm School Revisited*. Cambridge: Cambridge University Press, 1991, pp. 166 and 185–198, respectively.

**Unrefereed Articles**

"Technological Imperatives, Productivity and Insurance Costs." *The Geneva Papers on Risk and Insurance* 16, no. 58 (January 1991), pp. 1–12.

"Pricing in the UK Telecommunications Market: The Benefits of Competition." *Financial Times (of London)*, Wednesday, April 10, 1991, p. 13.

1990

**Books**

With Stephen M. Goldfeld, Lilli A. Gordon, and Michael F. Koehn. *The Economics of Mutual Fund Markets: Competition versus Regulation*. Norwell, Mass.: Kluwer, 1990, 256 pp.

## Chapter in Book

"Investimenti, Crescita della Popolazione e Stazionarieta di Tipo Ricardiano." Chapter 1 in S. Biasco, A. Roncaglia, and M. Salvati, eds., *Istituzioni e Mercato Nello Sviluppo Economico, Saggi in onore di Paolo Sylos Labini.* Roma-Bari: Gius. Laterza & Figli Spa, 1990, pp. 3–12.

## Refereed Articles

"Research on High School Economic Education: Discussion." *Journal of Economic Education* 21, no. 3 (Summer 1990), pp. 246–247.

"Productivity, Education and Feedback." *The Margin* 6, no. 1 (September/October 1990), p. 11.

"Entrepreneurship: Productive, Unproductive, and Destructive." *Journal of Political Economy* 98, no. 5, Part 1 (October 1990), pp. 893–921.

## Unrefereed Articles

"U.S. Industry's Lead Gets Bigger." *The Wall Street Journal,* March 21, 1990, p. A14.

"Erik Lundberg, 1907–1987." *Scandinavian Journal of Economics* 92(1), 1990, pp. 1–9.

"Quality Changes and Productivity Measurement: Hedonics and an Alternative." *Journal of Accounting, Auditing and Finance* 5, nos. 1/2 (N.S.) (Winter/Spring 1990), pp. 105–117.

## Review Article

Review of Denis Patrick O'Brien, *Lionel Robbins.* New York: St. Martin's Press, 1988, in *Journal of Economic Literature* XXVIII (March 1990), pp. 82–83.

## Other Publications

With Alexandre Rubinstein and Hilda Baumol. "On the Economics of the Performing Arts in the U.S.S.R. and the U.S.A.: A Preliminary Comparison of the Data." R.R.

90-36, (August 1990), C. V. Starr Center for Applied Economics, New York University.
"Beyond Allocative Efficiency: How Perfect Are the 'Perfect' Market Forms?" R.R. 90-37 (August 1990), C. V. Starr Center for Applied Economics, New York University.
"Technological Imperatives, Productivity and Insurance Costs." R.R. 90-35 (August 1990), C. V. Starr Center for Applied Economics, New York University.
"U.S. Economic Performance: We're Doing Better Than You Think." U.S. Treasury Bicentennial Closing Lecture, November 16, 1989, published in *Annual Report of the Treasury Historical Association*, U.S. Department of the Treasury Bicentennial Issue, 1989, pp. 27–29 (summary, biography, and photographs).
"Mergers and Megaculture." *University* 9, no. 2 (Fall 1990), New York University, p. 20.

1989

## Books
With Lars Osberg and Edward N. Wolff. *The Information Economy and the Implications of Unbalanced Growth*. Halifax, N.S.: Institute for Research on Public Policy, 1989, 114 pp.
With Sue Anne Batey Blackman and Edward N. Wolff. *Productivity and American Leadership: The Long View*. Cambridge: MIT Press, 1989, 395 pp.

## Chapters in Books
"On the Career of a Microeconomist." In J. A. Kregel, ed., *Recollections of Eminent Economists*, vol. 2. London: Macmillan, 1989, pp. 209–234.
"Lionel Robbins, 1898–1984." In David Greenaway and John R. Presley, eds., *Pioneers of Modern Economics in Britain*, vol. 2. London: Macmillan, 1989, pp. 11–23.

With Edward N. Wolff. "Three Fundamental Productivity Concepts: Principles and Measurement." In George R. Feiwel, ed., *Joan Robinson and Modern Economic Theory.* London: Macmillan, 1989, pp. 638–659.

Highlights from "Regulation, Litigation, and Misdirection of Entrepreneurship." In Mel G. Grinspan, *Celebrating the Wedding of Policy and Economics: A History of the Frank E. Seidman Distinguished Award in Political Economy.* Memphis, Tenn.: Rhodes College, 1989, pp. 78–81.

*Articles in Refereed Journals*

With Jess Benhabib. "Chaos: Significance, Mechanism, and Economic Applications." *Journal of Economic Perspectives* 3, no. 1 (Winter 1989), pp. 77–105.

"Is There a U.S. Productivity Crisis?" *Science* 243, no. 4891 (February 1989), pp. 611–615.

With James Tobin. "Communication. The Optimal Cash Balance Proposition: Maurice Allais' Priority." *Journal of Economic Literature* XXVII (September 1989), pp. 1160–1162.

*Article in Unrefereed Journal*

With Robert D. Willig. "Price Caps: A Rational Means to Protect Telecommunications Consumers and Competition." *Review of Business* 10, no. 4 (Spring 1989) (Business Research Institute, St. John's University, New York), pp. 3–8.

*Reviews*

"Views from Chicago," Review of George J. Stigler, *Memoirs of an Unregulated Economist.* In *Science* 245, no. 4923 (September 15, 1989), pp. 1259–1260.

*Other Article*

"Utility Commissioners' 'Innumeracy' Costs Plenty." *The Wall Street Journal*, November 8, 1989, p. A18.

1988

## Book

With Wallace E. Oates. *The Theory of Environmental Policy*, 2nd ed. Cambridge: Cambridge University Press, 1988, 299 pp.

With Alan S. Blinder. *Economics: Principles and Policy*, 4th ed. San Diego: Harcourt Brace Jovanovich, 1988, 926 pp.

## Chapters in Books

"Unpredictability, Pseudorandomness and Military–Civilian Budget Interactions." In Achille Agnati, Davide Cantarelli, and Aldo Montesno, eds., *Studi in Memoria di Tullio Bagiotti* (Essays in Memory of Tullio Bagiotti). Padova, Italy: Cedam, Casa Editrice Dott. Antonio Milani, 1988, pp. 143–145.

"On the Reality of Economic Illusion." In Sidney Hook, William L. O'Neill, and Roger O'Toole, eds., *Philosophy, History and Social Action, Essays in Honor of Lewis Feuer*. Dordrecht, Holland: Kluwer, 1988, pp. 103–117.

With Janusz A. Ordover. "Antitrust Policy and High-Technology Industries." *Oxford Review of Economic Policy* 4, no. 4 (Winter 1988).

## Articles in Refereed Journals

With Gerald R. Faulhaber. "Economists as Innovators: Practical Products of Theoretical Research." *Journal of Economic Literature* XXVI (June 1988), pp. 577–600.

With Edward N. Wolff. "Productivity Growth, Convergence, and Welfare: Reply." *American Economic Review* 78, no. 5 (December 1988), pp. 1155–1159.

## Other Articles

"Entrepreneurship: Productive, Unproductive and Imitative; or the Rule of the Rules of the Game." R.R. 88-07 (March 1988), C. V. Starr Center for Applied Economics, New York University.

With Janusz A. Ordover. "Antitrust Policy and High-Technology Industries." R.R. 88-25 (August 1988), C. V. Starr Center for Applied Economics, New York University.

"Containing Medical Costs: Why Price Controls Won't Work." *Public Interest* no. 93 (Fall 1988), pp. 37–53.

"Deindustrialization: Myth or Reality." *Senior Economist* 4, no. 1 (Fall 1988), pp. 3–4.

"Is Entrepreneurship Always Productive?" *Journal of Development Planning*, United Nations, no. 18, 1988.

"Economic Education and the Critics of Mainstream Economics." *Journal of Economic Education* 19, no. 4 (Fall 1988), pp. 232–330.

"After Reagan: The Laffer Curve Remains No Laughing Matter." *Entrepreneurship Forum*, Center of Entrepreneurial Studies, Leonard N. Stern School of Business, New York University (Winter 1988).

"Medicare Folly: Capping Doctors' Fees." *The New York Times*, December 27, 1988, p. A21.

1987

*Books*

With contributions by Dietrich Fischer. *Superfairness: Applications and Theory*, paper. ed. Cambridge: MIT Press, 1987, 266 pp.

With John C. Panzar and Robert D. Willig. *Contestable Markets and the Theory of Industry Structure*, rev. paper. ed. San Diego: Harcourt Brace Jovanovich, 1987, 538 pp.

*Chapters in Books*

With Dietrich Fischer. "Peak Pricing, Congestion and Fairness." In George R. Feiwel, ed., *Arrow and the Foun-*

*dations of the Theory of Economic Policy.* New York: New York University Press, 1987, pp. 382–409.

"Unnatural Value, or Art Investment as Floating Crap Game." In Douglas V. Shaw, William S. Hendon, and C. Richard Waits, eds., *Artists and Cultural Consumers.* Akron, Oh.: Association for Cultural Economics, 1987, pp. 1–21.

"Rebirth of a Fallen Leader: Italy and the Long Period Data." In Giancarlo Gandolfo and Ferruccio Marzano, eds., *Keynesian Theory Planning Models and Quantitative Economics, Essays in Memory of Vittorio Marrama*, vol. I. Milano: Dott. A. Giuffre Editore, 1987, pp. 135–160.

"Ramsey Pricing. Indivisibility. Economics of the Performing Arts." In John Eatwell, Murray Milgate, and Peter Newman, eds., *The New Palgrave: A Dictionary of Economics.* London: Macmillan, 1987.

## Articles in Refereed Journals

"Superfairness and Applied Microtheory." *Atlantic Economic Journal* XV, no. 1 (March 1987), p. 109.

"Entrepreneurship: Creative, Unproductive and Destructive." *Schweiz. Zeitschrift für Volkswirtschaft und Statistik* 3 (1987), pp. 415–423.

## Other Articles

"The Chaos Phenomenon: A Nightmare for Forecasters." *L.S.E. Quarterly* 1, no. 1 (March 1987), pp. 99–114.

"Microeconomics: A Comment on the Realism of Assumptions." *Journal of Economic Education* 18, no. 2 (Spring 1987), p. 155.

"America's Productivity 'Crisis': A Modest Decline Isn't All That Bad." *The New York Times*, February 15, 1987, Business Forum, p. 2.

With Robert D. Willig. "Using Competition as a Guide." *Regulation* no. 1, 1987, pp. 28–35.

With Michael F. Koehn and Robert D. Willig. "How Arbitrary Is 'Arbitrary'? – or, Toward the Deserved Demise of Full Cost Allocation." *Public Utilities Fortnightly* 120, no. 5 (September 3, 1987), pp. 16–21.

With Edward N. Wolff. "Three Fundamental Productivity Concepts: Principles and Measurement." Fishman-Davidson Center Discussion Paper, Wharton School, University of Pennsylvania, vol. 3 (Summer 1987).

With Edward N. Wolff. "Input and Output Composition Changes: Measuring the Effect on the Productivity Slowdown." Fishman-Davidson Discussion Paper, Wharton School, University of Pennsylvania, vol. 3 (Summer 1987).

"A Conversation with William J. Baumol About Productivity Growth." *Eastern Economic Journal* XIII, no. 3 (July–September 1987), pp. 189–192.

"Entrepreneurship: An Historical Overview." *On Aspects of Entrepreneurship*, Price Institute for Entrepreneurial Studies booklet (1987), pp. 6–12.

"Lionel Charles, Lord Robbins of Clare Market (22 November 1898–15 May 1984)." *American Philosophical Society Memorials* (1987), pp. 161–163.

"Regulation, Litigation, and Misdirection of Entrepreneurship." Acceptance paper for the Frank E. Seidman Distinguished Award in Political Economy, Memphis, Tenn., September 17, 1987. Memphis: P. K. Seidman Foundation, October 1987, pp. 1–13.

With Edward N. Wolff. "Is International Productivity Convergence Illusory?" R.R. 87-38 (September 1987), C. V. Starr Center for Applied Economics, New York University.

*Reprints*

"La valeur antinaturelle ou l'investissement, dans les oeuvres d'art considéré comme un coup de poker." *Proceedings of Conference*, "Les outils de l'économiste à l'épreuve," 1987, pp. 31–44. (Reprint of "Unnatural Value, or Art Investment as Floating Crap Game.")

1986

### Books
With contributions by Dietrich Fischer. *Superfairness: Applications and Theory.* Cambridge: MIT Press, 1986, 266 pp.

*Microtheory: Applications and Origins.* Cambridge: MIT Press; and Brighton, England: Wheatsheaf Books, 1986, 286 pp.

*Economics: Principles and Policy,* 3rd ed. *Microeconomics* (with Alan S. Blinder). New York: Harcourt Brace Jovanovich, 1986.

### Chapters in Books
With J. C. Panzar and R. D. Willig. "On the Theory of Perfectly Contestable Markets." In *New Developments in the Analysis of Market Structure,* ed. by Joseph E. Stiglitz and G. Frank Mathewson, Cambridge: MIT Press, 1986, pp. 339–365.

Chapter 8, "Information Technology and the Service Sector: A Feedback Process?" and Chapter 9, "Conclusion." In Gerald Faulhaber, Eli Noam, and Roberta Tasley, eds., *Services in Transition: The Impact of Information Technology on the Service Sector.* Cambridge, Mass.: Ballinger, 1986, pp. 183–199.

### Articles in Refereed Journals
"Unnatural Value: Or, Art Investment as Floating Crap Game." *American Economic Association Papers and Proceedings: Economic Issues in the Arts* 76, no. 2 (May 1986), pp. 10–14.

"On the Possibility of Continuing Expansion of Finite Resources." *Kyklos* 39, fasc. 2 (1986), pp. 167–179.

"Productivity Growth, Convergence, and Welfare: What the Long-Run Data Show." *American Economic Review* 76, no. 5 (December 1986), pp. 1072–1085.

*Review Articles*

Review of Angus Maddison, *Phases of Capitalist Development.* In *Journal of Economic Literature* XXIV (June 1986), pp. 689–690.

Review of Oliver E. Williamson, *The Economic Institutions of Capitalism.* In *Rand Journal of Economics* 17, no. 2 (Summer 1986), pp. 279–286.

*Other Articles*

"The Lesson of Long-Term Productivity Trends." *Economic Impact* no. 54 (1986/2), pp. 78–83.

With Kenneth McLennan. "Are We on the Downward Path the British Took?" *Washington Post*, April 24, 1986.

"Unpredictability, Pseudorandomness and Military–Civilian Budget Interactions (Imprevedibilità, pseudocasualità e interazioni tra preventivi di spesa militare e civile)." *Revista Internazionale di Scienze Economiche e Commerciali* XXXIII, no. 4 (April 1986), pp. 297–318.

With Janusz A. Ordover. "Use of Antitrust to Subvert Competition." *Journal of Reprints for Antitrust Law and Economics* XVI, no. 2 (1986), pp. 649–669 (reprinted from *Journal of Law and Economics* XXVIII (May 1986), pp. 247–265.

With Sue Anne Batey Blackman and Edward N. Wolff. "Nouvel Examen du Modele de Croissance Déséquilibrée: Application au Cas Américain." *Problèmes Économiques, Sélection de Textes Français et Étrangers* (16 April 1986), no. 1.970, pp. 14–22 (reprint of "Unbalanced Growth Revisited: Asymptotic Stagnancy and New Evidence." *American Economic Review* 75, no. 4 (September 1985), pp. 806–817).

"On Contestable Market Analysis." Conference Board Research Bulletin no. 195, *Antitrust and New Views of Microeconomics* (1986), pp. 13–14.

"Entrepreneurship and the Long-Run Productivity Record." R.R. 86-04 (February 1986), C. V. Starr Center for Applied Economics, New York University.

"Information, Business and Productivity Growth." *Proceedings of the 1986 International Conference on Economics and Management.* Tokyo: IBM Japan, 1986, pp. 18–30.

"J. B. Say and the 'Traité.'" Introduction to 1986 edition of Jean-Baptiste Say, *Traité d'Économie Politique.* Düsseldorf: Verlag Wirtschaft und Finanzen GMBH, ein unternehmen der Verlagsgruppe Handelsblatt, 1986, pp. 15–53.

With Robert D. Willig. "Contestability: Developments Since the Book." *Oxford Economic Papers Special Issue, Strategic Behavior and Industrial Competition*, D. J. Morris, P. J. N. Sinclair, M. D. E. Slater, and J. S. Vickers, eds. Oxford: Clarendon Press (November 1986), pp. 9–36.

1985

*Books*

Ed. with Kenneth McLennan. *Productivity Growth and U.S. Competitiveness.* New York: Oxford University Press, 1985, 228 pp.

With Alan S. Blinder. *Economics: Principles and Policy*, 3rd ed. San Diego: Harcourt Brace Jovanovich, 1985, 893 pp.

With Alan S. Blinder and William M. Scarth. *Economics: Principles and Policy*, Canadian ed. Toronto: Academic Press, 1985, 874 pp.

*Chapters in Books*

With Hilda Baumol. "The Future of the Theater and the Cost Disease of the Arts." In *Bach and the Box: The Impact of Television on the Live Arts*, ed. by Mary Ann Hendon, James F. Richardson, and William A. Hendon. Akron, Oh.: Association for Cultural Economics, 1985, pp. 7–31.

With Hilda Baumol. "On the Cost Disease and Its True Policy Implications for the Arts." In *Public Choice, Public Finance and Public Policy*, ed. by David Greenaway and G. K. Shaw. London: Basil Blackwell, 1985, pp. 67–77.

"Industry Structure Analysis and Public Policy." In *Issues in Contemporary Microeconomics and Welfare*, ed. by George R. Feiwel. London: Macmillan, 1985, pp. 311–327.

With Kenneth McLennan. "U.S. Productivity Performance and Its Implications." In *Productivity Growth and U.S. Competitiveness*, ed. by William J. Baumol and Kenneth McLennan. New York: Oxford University Press, 1985, pp. 3–28.

With Kenneth McLennan. "Toward an Effective Productivity Program." In *Productivity Growth and U.S. Competitiveness*, ed. by William J. Baumol and Kenneth McLennan. New York: Oxford University Press, 1985, pp. 187–224.

With Hilda Baumol. L'Avenir du Théâtre et le problème descouts du spectacle vivant. In *L'Économie du Spectacle Vivant et l'Audiovisuel*. Proceedings of Colloque International, Nice, October 1984, published by Ministère de la Culture Service des Études et Recherches and the Association pour Développement et la Diffusion de l'Économie de la Culture.

*Refereed Articles and Reviews*

With Sue Anne Batey Blackman and Edward N. Wolff. "Unbalanced Growth Revisited: Asymptotic Stagnancy and New Evidence." *American Economic Review* 75, no. 4 (September 1985), pp. 806–817.

With Richard E. Quandt. "Chaos Models and Their Implications for Forecasting." *Eastern Economic Journal* XI, no. 1 (January–March 1985), pp. 3–15.

With Janusz A. Ordover. "Use of Antitrust to Subvert Competition." *Journal of Law and Economics* XXVIII, no. 2 (May 1985), pp. 247–265.

## Other Articles

"Obituary: Lionel Robbins, 1898–1984." *Economica* 52, no. 205 (February 1985), pp. 5–7.

"Productivity Policy and the Service Sector." *Wharton Annual* (1985), pp. 46–54.

With Robert D. Willig. "Telephones and Computers: The Costs of Artificial Separation." *Regulation* 9 (March/April 1985), pp. 23–32.

"U.S. Productivity Growth: History as Antidote to Both Hysteria and Complacency." *Social Education* 49, no. 7 (October 1985), pp. 568–570.

"Unnatural Value: Or Art Investment as Floating Crap Game," R.R. 85-25 (August 1985), C. V. Starr Center for Applied Economics, New York University.

"Unpredictability, Pseudorandomness and Military–Civilian Budget Interactions." R.R. 85-24 (August 1985), C. V. Starr Center for Applied Economics, New York University.

"Rebirth of a Fallen Leader: Italy and the Long-Period Data." R.R. 85-22 (June 1985), C. V. Starr Center for Applied Economics, New York University.

"Panel Discussion: Public Support for the Arts." From Symposium on the Public Benefits of the Arts and Humanities." *Art and the Law* 9, no. 2 (1985), pp. 214–228.

"Productivity Growth, Convergence and Welfare: What the Long Run Data Show." R.R. 85-27 (August 1985), C. V. Starr Center for Applied Economics, New York University.

"On Method in Economics: A Century Earlier." R.R. 85-28 (September 1985), C. V. Starr Center for Applied Economics, New York University.

"On the Possibility of Continuing Expansion of Finite

Resources." R.R. 85-29 (September 1985), C. V. Starr Center for Applied Economics, New York University.

With Edwin S. Mills. "Paying Companies to Obey the Law." *The New York Times*, Forum, October 27, 1985, p. F3.

"Productivity and the Service Sector." In *Managing the Service Economy*, ed. by Robert P. Inman. New York: Cambridge University Press, 1985, pp. 301–317.

"Rebirth of a Fallen Leader: Italy and the Long Period Data." *Atlantic Economic Journal* XIII, no. 3 (September 1985), pp. 12–26.

"Unnatural Value: Or Art Investment as Floating Crap Game." *Journal of Arts Management and Law* 15, no. 3 (Fall 1985), pp. 47–59.

"On Method in U.S. Economics a Century Earlier." *American Economic Review* 75, no. 6 (December 1985), pp. 1–12.

*Interview*

On Productivity, Competition, and Marmalade. *The Margin* 1, no. 3 (December 1985), pp. 3–5.


1984


*Book*

Editor with Hilda Baumol, *Inflation and the Performing Arts*. New York: New York University Press, 1984, 210 pp.

*Chapters in Books*

"Matching Private Incentives to Public Goals." Chapter 8 in *Public-Private Partnership, New Opportunities for Meeting Social Needs*, ed. by Harvey Brooks, Lance Liebman, and

Corinne S. Schelling. Cambridge, Mass.: Ballinger, 1984, pp. 175–194.

With Wallace E. Oates. "Long-Run Trends in Environmental Quality." Chapter 16 in *The Resourceful Earth: A Response to Global 2000*, ed. by Julian L. Simon and Herman Kahn. Oxford: Basil Blackwell, 1984, pp. 439–475 (reprint).

With Sue Anne Batey Blackman. "Electronics, the Cost Disease and the Operation of Libraries." In *Library Lit. vol. 14 – The Best of 1983*, ed. by Bill Katz. Metuchen, N.J.: Scarecrow Press, 1984, pp. 3–24 (reprint).

Foreword. In *An Essay on the Nature and Significance of Economic Science*, 3rd ed., Lord Robbins. London: Macmillan, 1984, pp. vii–ix.

With Edward N. Wolff. "Feedback Models: R&D, Information, and Productivity Growth." In *Communication and Information Economics: New Perspectives*, ed. by Meheroo Jussawalla and Helene Ebenfield. Amsterdam: Elsevier, North-Holland, 1984, pp. 73–93.

With Edward N. Wolff. "Feedback from Productivity Growth to R&D." In *Topics in Production Theory*, ed. by Finn R. Førsund. New York: Macmillan, 1984.

With Hilda Baumol. "The Mass Media and the Cost Disease." In *The Economics of Cultural Industries*, ed. by William S. Hendon, Douglas V. Shaw, and Nancy K. Grant. Akron, Oh.: Association for Cultural Economics, 1984, pp. 109–123.

With Hilda Baumol. "The Family of the Arts. On the Finances of Off-Broadway and Other Small Theatres. On Inflation and the Arts: A Summing Up." In *Inflation and the Performing Arts*, ed. by Hilda Baumol and William J. Baumol. New York: New York University Press, 1984, pp. 3–24, 56–70, 173–195.

Contribution. In *Tributes in Memory of Lord Robbins, C.H., C.B.*, presented October 11, 1984, London, pp. 10–11.

*Refereed Articles and Reviews*

With Edward N. Wolff. "On Interindustry Differences in Absolute Productivity." *Journal of Political Economy* 92, no. 6 (December 1984), pp. 1017–1034.

Review of *Paul Samuelson and Modern Economic Theory*, ed. by E. Cary Brown and Robert M. Solow. *Journal of Economic Literature* XXII (March 1984), pp. 92–93.

*Other Articles*

With Elizabeth E. Bailey. "Deregulation and the Theory of Contestable Markets." *Yale Journal on Regulation* 1, no. 2 (1984), pp. 111–137.

"Toward a Theory of Public Enterprise." *Atlantic Economic Journal* XII, no. 1 (March 1984), pp. 13–19.

"On Productivity Growth in the Long Run." *Atlantic Economic Journal* XII, no. 3 (September 1984), pp. 5–10.

With Sue Anne Batey Blackman and Edward N. Wolff. "Unbalanced Growth Revisited: Asymptotic Stagnancy and New Evidence." R.R. 84-02 (January 1984), C. V. Starr Center for Applied Economics, New York University.

"U.S. Competitiveness and the Productivity Gap." *Journal of Economic Education* 15, no. 3 (Summer 1984), pp. 217–224.

With Edwin S. Mills. "Incentives for Solving Social Problems." *Challenge* 27, no. 5 (November–December 1984), pp. 47–53.

"Productivity Policy and the Service Sector." Discussion Paper no.1, Fishman-Davidson Center for the Study of the Service Sector, Wharton School, University of Pennsylvania, April 1984.

With Hilda Baumol. "In Culture, the Cost Disease Is Contagious." *The New York Times*, June 3, 1984, Section 2, pp. 1, 36.

*Book*

With Alan S. Blinder. *Economics: Principles and Policy*, 2nd ed. San Diego: Harcourt Brace Jovanovich, 1982, 836 pp.

*Chapters in Books*

Preface and Chapter 3, "Toward Operational Models of Entrepreneurship." In *Entrepreneurship*, ed. by Joshua Ronen. Lexington, Mass.: Lexington Books, D. C. Heath, 1983, pp. ix–x, 29–48.

"Entrepreneurship and the Sociopolitical Climate." In *Entrepreneurship and the Outlook for America*, ed. by Jules Backman. New York: Free Press, 1983, pp. 174–192.

"Minimum and Maximum Pricing Principles for Residual Regulation." In *Current Issues in Public-Utility Economics*, ed. by Albert L. Danielsen and David R. Kamerschen. Lexington, Mass.: D. C. Heath, 1983, pp. 177–196.

"Natural Monopoly and Contestable Market Analysis." In *State Enterprise and Deregulation*, Centre of Policy Studies, Monash University, Special Study no. 5, 1983.

*Refereed Articles*

"Marx and the Iron Law of Wages." *American Economic Review, Papers and Proceedings* 73, no. 2 (May 1983), pp. 303–308.

With Sue Anne Batey Blackman. "Electronics, the Cost Disease, and the Operation of Libraries." *Journal of the American Society for Information Science* 34, no. 3 (May 1983), pp. 181–191.

With John C. Panzar and Robert D. Willig. "Contestable Markets: An Uprising in the Theory of Industry Structure:

Reply." *American Economic Review* 73, no. 3 (June 1983), pp. 491–496.

## Book Review

Review of *An Evolutionary Theory of Economic Change,* by Richard R. Nelson and Sidney G. Winter. In *Journal of Economic Literature* XXI (June 1983), pp. 580–581.

## Other Articles

With Martin Shubik and Peggy Heim. "On Contracting with Publishers: Authors' Information Updated." *American Economic Review, Papers and Proceedings* 73, no. 2 (May 1983), pp. 365–381.

"In Memoriam: Fritz Machlup 1902–1983." *Academe: Bulletin of the AAUP* 69, no. 3 (May–June 1983), pp. 69–70.

"Some Subtle Pricing Issues in Railroad Regulation." *International Journal of Transport Economics* X, nos. 1–2 (April–August 1983), pp. 341–355.

With Edward N. Wolff. "Feedback from Productivity Growth to R&D." *Scandinavian Journal of Economics* 85, no. 2 (1983), pp. 147–157.

"On the Career of a Microeconomist." *Banca Nazionale del Lavoro Quarterly Review* no. 147 (December 1983), pp. 311–335.

"Professor Ahsan and the Social Rate of Discount: A Reply." *Public Finance* 38, no. 3, 1983, pp. 465–467.

1981–1982

## Books

With Robert D. Willig and John C. Panzar. *Contestable Markets and the Theory of Industry Structure.* San Diego: Harcourt Brace Jovanovich, 1982, 510 pp.

With Alan S. Blinder. *Economics: Principles and Policy*, 2nd ed. San Diego: Harcourt Brace Jovanovich, 1982, 836 pp.

Chapters in Books

"Technological Change and the New Urban Equilibrium." In *Cities Under Stress: The Fiscal Crisis of Urban America*, ed. by Robert W. Burchell and David Listokin. Piscataway, N.J.: Center for Urban Policy Research, Rutgers University, 1981, pp. 3–17.

Comments on Kenneth C. Baseman's *Open Entry and Cross-Subsidization in Regulated Markets*. In *Studies in Public Regulation*, ed. by Gary Fromm. Cambridge: MIT Press, 1981, pp. 361–364.

"Planning and Dual Values of Linearized Nonlinear Problems: A Gothic Tale." In *The Theory and Experience of Economic Development: Essays in Honor of Sir W. Arthur Lewis*, ed. by Mark Gersovitz, Carlos F. Diaz-Alejandro, Gustav Ranis, and Mark R. Rosenzweig. London: George Allen and Unwin, 1982, pp. 275–284.

Refereed Articles

With Robert D. Willig. "Fixed Costs, Sunk Costs, Entry Barriers, Public Goods, and Sustainability of Monopoly." *Quarterly Journal of Economics* XCVI, no. 3 (August 1981), pp. 405–431.

With Edward Wolff. "Subsidies to New Energy Sources: Do They Add to Energy Stocks?" *Journal of Political Economy* 89, no. 5 (October 1981), pp. 891–913.

"Applied Fairness Theory and Rationing Policy." *American Economic Review* 72, no. 4 (September 1982), pp. 639–651.

"Contestable Markets: An Uprising in the Theory of Industry Structure." *American Economic Review* 72, no. 1 (March 1982), pp. 1–15.

*Other Articles*

"Some Principles for the Operation of Public Enterprises." *Academia Economic Papers* 9, no. 1 (March 1981), pp. 69–79.

"On My Sculptures of Carved Wood." *Leonardo: International Journal of the Contemporary Artist* 15, no. 1 (1982), pp. 40–42.

With Sue Anne Batey Blackman. "The Importance of Energy Profitability." *Economic Impact* 1, no. 37 (1982), pp. 15–20.

"The Income Distribution Frontier and Taxation of Migrants." *Journal of Public Economics* 18, no. 3 (August 1982), pp. 343–361.

"Productivity Incentive Clauses and Rate Adjustment for Inflation." *Public Utilities Fortnightly* 110, no. 2 (July 22, 1982), pp. 11–18.

With Martin Shubik and Peggy Heim. "On Contracting with Publishers: Information for Authors Updated." Prepared for Executive Committee, American Economic Association, September 1982.

"Contestable Markets, Antitrust and Regulation." *Wharton Magazine* 7, no. 1 (Fall 1982), pp. 23–30.

With Robert D. Willig. "International Failures of the Invisible Hand: Theory and Implications for International Market Dominance." *Indian Economic Review* XVI, nos. 1, 2 (January–June 1981), pp. 1–12.

*Book Reviews*

With Hilda Baumol. Review of *The Economics of the Performing Arts*, by C. D. Throsby and G. A. Withers. *Journal of Political Economy* 89, no. 2 (April 1981), p. 425.

Review of *What Price Incentives?: Economists and the Environment*, by Steven Kelman. *Journal of Economic Literature* XX (September 1982), pp. 115–116.

1980

## Book

Editor. *Public and Private Enterprise in a Mixed Economy.*
Proceedings of International Economic Association
Conference, Mexico City. London: Macmillan, 1980, 308
pp.

## Articles

With Hilda Baumol. "Financial Prospects for the Performing Arts: Report from the Cloudy Crystal Ball." *ACUCAA
Bulletin,* no. 78 (March 1980) (Supplement).

With Sue Anne Batey Blackman. "Unprofitable Energy Is
Squandered Energy." *Challenge* 23, no. 3 (July/August),
1980, pp. 28–35.

"Theory of Equity in Pricing for Resource Conservation."
*Journal of Environmental Economics and Management* 7,
no. 4 (December 1980), pp. 308–320.

With Sue Anne Batey Blackman. "Modified Fiscal Incentives in Environmental Policy." *Land Economics* 56, no. 4
(November 1980), pp. 417–431.

With Y. M. Braunstein. "The Economics of R and D."
*Management Science* 15 (1980).

With Hilda Baumol. "On Finances of the Performing Arts
During Stagflation: Some Recent Data." *Journal of Cultural Economics* 4, no. 2 (December 1980), pp. 1–14.

With Wallace E. Oates. "The Cost Disease of the Personal
Services and the Quality of Life." In *Teoria de la Democracia:
Una Approximacion Economica,* ed. by A. C. Vinardell.
Madrid: Instituto de Estudios Fiscales, 1980, pp. 461–484
(reprint).

*Teoria economica y analisis de operaciones.* Trans. by Alfredo
Roa. Madrid: Editorial Dossat, S.A., 1980, 701 pp. (trans.).

1979

*Book*
With Alan S. Blinder. *Economics: Principles and Policy.* New York: Harcourt Brace Jovanovich, 1979, 862 pp.

*Chapters in Books*
"Pricing Devices to Aid the Invisible Hand." In *The Political Economy of Policy-Making: Essays in Honor of Will E. Mason,* ed. by M. P. Dooley, H. M. Kaufman, and R. E. Lombra. Beverly Hills, Calif.: Sage Publications, 1979, pp. 117–128.
"On Two Experiments in the Pricing of Theater Tickets." In *Economics and Human Welfare: Essays in Honor of Tibor Scitovsky,* ed. by M. J. Boskin. New York: Academic Press, 1979, pp. 41–57.
With F. R. Edwards. Discussion of Part 3: "Problems of Efficiency and Competition." In *Impending Changes for Securities Markets: What Role for the Exchanges?* ed. by E. Bloch and R. A. Schwartz. Greenwich, Conn.: Jai Press, 1979, pp. 194–202.
With E. V. Seiler. "Viner, Jacob." In *International Encyclopedia of the Social Sciences, Biographical Supplement,* vol. 18, ed. by David L. Sills. New York: Free Press, 1979, pp. 783–787.
Discussion of William Schuman and R. L. Stevens. In *Economic Pressures and the Future of the Arts.* New York: Free Press, 1979.
"On Some Microeconomic Issues in Inflation Theory." In *Essays in Post-Keynesian Inflation,* ed. by J. H. Gapinski and C. E. Rockwood. Cambridge, Mass.: Ballinger, 1979, pp. 55–78.

*Articles*

"On the Folklore of Marxism." *Proceedings of the American Philosophical Society* 123, no. 2 (April 1979), pp. 124–128.

With Dietrich Fischer and Thijs ten Raa. "The Price-Iso Return Locus and Rational Rate Regulation." *Bell Journal of Economics* 10, no. 2 (Autumn 1979), pp. 648–658.

"Quasi-Optimality: The Price We Must Pay for a Price System." *Journal of Political Economy* 87, no. 3 (June 1979), pp. 578–599.

With Dietrich Fischer. "The Output Distribution Frontier: Alternatives to Income Taxes and Transfers for Strong Equality Goals." *American Economic Review* 69, no. 4 (September 1979), pp. 514–525.

"On the Contributions of Herbert A. Simon to Economics." *Scandinavian Journal of Economics* 81, no. 1 (1979), pp. 74–82.

"Minimum and Maximum Pricing Principles for Residual Regulation." *Eastern Economic Journal* 5, nos. 1–2 (January–April 1979), pp. 235–248.

"Quasi-Permanence of Price Reductions: A Policy for Prevention of Predatory Pricing." *Yale Law Journal* 89, no. 1 (November 1979), pp. 1–26.

With M. B. Krauss. "Guest Workers and Income Transfer Programs Financed by Host Governments." *Kyklos* 32, fasc. 1/2 (1979), pp. 36–46.

"On Conservation of Energy and Use of the Market Mechanism." In *Energy and Community Development*, Proceedings of National Energy Council of Greece and U.S. Department of Energy Conference, Athens, 1979, pp. 277–294.

*Other Publication*

Foreword: *Some Insufficiencies in the Theories of International Economic Relations*, by Bertil Ohlin. In *Essays in Interna-*

*tional Finance*, no. 134 (September 1979). Princeton: Princeton University, Department of Economics, International Finance Section, pp. v, vi.

*Book Review*

Review of Roman Rosdolsky, *The Making of Marx's "Capital."* In *Journal of Political Economy* 87, no. 1 (February 1979), pp. 220–223.

1978

*Book*

With Wallace E. Oates and Sue Anne Batey Blackman. *Economics, Environmental Policy, and the Quality of Life.* Englewood Cliffs, N.J.: Prentice-Hall, 1979, 377 pp. (released September 1978).

*Chapters in Books*

"On the Stochastic Unemployment Distribution Model and the Long-Run Phillips Curve." In A. R. Bergstrom et al., eds. *Stability and Inflation, Essays in Honour of Professor A. W. H. Phillips.* New York: John Wiley, 1978, pp. 3–20.

"Consumers' and Producers' Surplus vs. Externality Effects of Innovation." In T. Bagiotti and G. Franco, eds. *Pioneering Economics, International Essays in Honor of Giovanni Demaria.* Padua, Italy: Cedam, 1978, pp. 43–58.

"The Transformation of Values: What Marx `Really' Meant (An Interpretation)," in Paul M. Sweezy et al., eds., *The Transformation Problem.* Tokyo: University of Tokyo Press, 1978, pp. 137–59.

With Dietrich Fischer. "Optimal Lags in a Schumpeterian Innovation Process." In Jacob S. Dreyer, ed., *Breadth and Depth in Economics: Essays in Honor of Fritz Machlup.* Lexington, Mass.: D. C. Heath, 1978, pp. 241–270.

"Smith vs. Marx on Business Morality and the Social Interest." In Fred R. Glahe, ed., *Adam Smith and the Wealth of Nations, 1776–1976 Bicentennial Essays* (Boulder: Colorado Associated University Press, 1978), pp. 111–122.

*Articles*

With Dietrich Fischer. "Cost Minimizing Number of Firms and Determination of Industry Structure." *Quarterly Journal of Economics* (August 1978), pp. 439–467.

"The Adam Smith That Nobody Knows." *MBA* 12, no. 4 (April 1978), pp. 34–36.

"Equity vs. Allocative Efficiency: Toward a Theory of Distributive Justice." *Atlantic Economic Journal* 6, no. 1 (March 1978), pp. 8–16.

*Book Review*

Review of Gary Becker, *The Economic Approach to Human Behavior.* In *Economica* (August 1978), pp. 313–315.

1977

*Books*

*Economic Theory and Operations Analysis,* 4th ed. Englewood Cliffs, N.J.: Prentice-Hall, 1977, 695 pp.

Editor and author of portions. *Noise Abatement: Policy Alternatives for Transportation.* Washington, D.C.: National Research Council, National Academy of Sciences, 1977, 232 pp.

*Articles*

With Yale M. Braunstein. "Empirical Study of Scale Economies and Production Complementarity: The Case of

Journal Publication." *Journal of Political Economy* 85, no. 5 (1977), pp. 1037–1048.

"The Public Good Attribute as Independent Justification for Subsidy." *Intermountain Economic Review* 8, no. 2 (Fall 1977), pp. 1–10.

"On the Proper Cost Tests for Natural Monopoly in a Multiproduct Industry." *American Economic Review* 67, no. 5 (December 1977), pp. 809–822.

With Elizabeth E. Bailey and Robert D. Willig. "Weak Invisible Hand Theorems on the Sustainability of Multi-Product Natural Monopoly." *American Economic Review* 67, no. 3 (June 1977), pp. 350–365.

"On Recycling as a Moot Environmental Issue." *Journal of Environmental Economics and Management* 4 (1977), pp. 83–87.

With J. A. Ordover. "On the Optimality of Public-Goods Pricing with Exclusion Devices." *Kyklos* 30, fasc. 1 (1977), pp. 5–21.

"Say's (at Least) Eight Laws, or What Say and James Mill May Really Have Meant." *Economica* 44 (May 1977), pp. 145–162.

With Hilda Baumol. "The Impact of the Broadway Theatre on the Economy of New York City." New York: League of New York Theatres and Producers, 1977, 49 pp.

With Y. M. Braunstein, D. M. Fischer, and J. A. Ordover. *Manual of Pricing and Cost Determination for Organizations Engaged in Dissemination of Knowledge. Report to Division of Science Information of the National Science Foundation* (April 1977).

1975–1976

*Book*

*Selected Economic Writings of William J. Baumol*, ed. by Elizabeth E. Bailey. New York: New York University Press, 1976.

## Chapters in Books

With William G. Bowen. "Recent Developments in the Economics of the Performing Arts," preface, *The Economics of the Arts*, Mark Blaug, ed. London: Martin Robertson, 1976, pp. 1–12.

With William G. Bowen. "Arguments for Public Support of the Performing Arts." Chapter 2, *The Economics of the Arts*, Mark Blaug, ed. London: Martin Robertson, 1976, pp. 42–57.

With William G. Bowen. "A Survey of American and British Audiences for the Performing Arts." Chapter 9, *The Economics of the Arts*, Mark Blaug, ed. London: Martin Robertson, 1976, pp. 148–172.

With William G. Bowen. "On the Performing Arts: The Anatomy of Their Economic Problems." Chapter 13, *The Economics of the Arts*, Mark Blaug, ed. London: Martin Robertson, 1976, pp. 218–226.

With Wallace E. Oates. "Conservation of Resources and the Price System." *Economics of Resources*, Robert D. Leiter and Stanley L. Friedlander, eds., New York: Cyrco Press, 1976, pp. 15–35.

"On International Issues in Environmental Management." *Studies in International Environmental Economics*, Ingo Walters, ed. New York: John Wiley, 1976, pp. 1–8.

"Scale Economies, Average Cost and the Profitability of Marginal Cost Pricing." *Public and Urban Economics: Essays in Honor of William S. Vickrey*, R. E. Grieson, ed. Lexington, Mass: D. C. Heath, 1976.

"On the Theory and Practice of Discount-Factor Calculation in Cost-Benefit Analysis. Presented at US/USSR Conference on the Economics of Information Dissemination, Leningrad, 1976 (published in Russian).

## Articles and Miscellaneous Papers

With J. A. Ordover. "On the Optimality of Public Goods Pricing with Exclusion Devices." New York University,

Center for Applied Economics, Discussion Paper 75-49, November 1975.

With Elizabeth E. Bailey and Robert D. Willig. "Weak Invisible Hand Theorems on Pricing and Entry in a Multi-Product Monopoly." New York University, Center for Applied Economics, Discussion Paper 75-50, November 1975.

With D. Fischer. "On the Optimal Number of Firms in an Industry." New York University, Center for Applied Economics, Discussion Paper 75-51, November 1975.

With Y. Braunstein. "Scale Economies, Production Complementarity and Information Distribution by Scientific Journals." New York University, Center for Applied Economics, Discussion Paper 75-05, 1976.

"It Takes Two to Tango, or Sind `Separable Externalities' Überhaupt Möglich?" *Journal of Political Economy* 84, no. 2 (April 1976), pp. 381–388.

"Economic Counseling in State Government." *8th Annual Report, Economic Policy Council and Office of Economic Policy*, Department of the Treasury, State of New Jersey, Trenton, September 1975, pp. 23–26.

"Smith vs. Marx on Business Morality and the Social Interest." *American Economist* 20, no. 1 (Spring 1976), pp. 1–6.

## Reviews

Review of Gerard Maarek, *Introduction au Capital de Karl Marx*, in *Journal of Economic Literature* XIV, no. 1 (March 1976), pp. 82–88.

Review of Bruce A. Ackerman and Susan Rose-Ackerman, James W. Sawyer, Jr., and Dale W. Henderson. *The Uncertain Search for Environmental Quality*. In *Yale Law Journal* 85, no. 3 (January 1976), pp. 441–446.

## Books

With Wallace E. Oates. *The Theory of Environmental Policy: Externalities, Public Outlays and the Quality of Life.* Englewood Cliffs, N.J.: Prentice-Hall, 1975, 272 pp.

With Hilda Baumol. *Last-Minute Discounts on Unsold Tickets: A Study of TKTS, Report I.* New York: Theatre Development Fund, 1974, 53 pp.

*Economic Dynamics*, 2nd ed. Greek translation. Athens: Editions Papazissis, 1974.

## Chapters in Books

"Environmental Protection and Income Distribution," Chapter 4 in Harold M. Hochman and George E. Peterson, eds., *Redistribution Through Public Choice.* New York: Columbia University Press, 1974, pp. 93–114.

"Economic Utility and Value." In *Encyclopaedia Britannica*, 15th ed. London: Encyclopaedia Britannica, 1974, pp. 3–8.

"Business Responsibility and Economic Behavior." In Edmund S. Phelps, ed., *Altruism, Morality and Economic Theory.* New York: Russell Sage Foundation, 1975, pp. 45–56.

"Acceleration Incentives and X-Efficiency." In Willy Sallekaerts, ed., *Econometrics and Economic Theory: Essays in Honour of Jan Tinbergen.* London: Macmillan, 1974, pp. 167–175.

"Scale Economies, Average Cost and the Profitability of Marginal Cost Pricing." In Ronald E. Grieson, ed., *Essays in Urban Economics and Public Finance in Honor of William S. Vickrey.* Lexington, Mass.: D. C. Heath, 1975.

"On the Stochastic Unemployment Distribution Model and the Long-Run Phillips Curve." For *Essays in Honour of A. W. Phillips*, presented November 1974, Hamilton, N.Z.

*Pamphlets*

"Say's (at Least) Eight Laws, or What Say and James Mill May Really Have Meant." New York University, Center for Applied Economics, November 1974, no. 74-22, 25 pp.

"On the Proper Cost Tests for Natural Monopoly in a Multi-Product Industry." New York University, Center for Applied Economics, May 1975, no. 75-35, 32 pp.

"Scale Economies, Average Cost and the Profitability of Marginal Cost Pricing." New York University, Center for Applied Economics, May 1975, no. 75-34, 18 pp.

"On Two Experiments in the Pricing of Theatre Tickets," for Theatre Development Fund of New York and Mathematica, Inc., Princeton, 1975, 24 pp.

*Articles*

"On Taxation and the Control of Externalities: Reply." *American Economic Review* LXIV, no. 3 (June 1974), p. 472.

With M. Oates. "On the Economics of the Theatre in Renaissance London and Gay Nineties Eldora: Reply." *Swedish Journal of Economics* 6, no. 3 (1974).

"Payment by Performance in Rail Passenger Transportation: An Innovation in Amtrak's Operations." *Bell Journal of Economics* 6, no. 1 (Spring 1975), pp. 281–298.

"On the Appropriate Discount Rate for Evaluation of Public Projects." *African Administrative Studies*, no. 13 (January 1975), pp. 161–168.

*Reviews*

Review of A. Sen, *On Economic Inequality*. In *Economica*, 55 (1975), p. 6.

Review of Michio Morishima, *Marx's Economics: A Dual Theory of Value and Growth*. In *Monthly Review* 26, no. 9 (February 1975), pp. 57–64.

1973–1974

## Books

With M. Marcus. *Economics of Academic Libraries.* Washington, D.C.: American Council on Education (1973), 98 pp.

## Chapter in Book

"Business Responsibility and Economic Behavior." Chapter 4 in Melvin Anshen, ed., *Managing the Socially Responsible Corporation.* New York: Macmillan, 1974, pp. 59–70.

## Articles

With T. Fabian. "Comments on Maiti and Sengupta's Note." *Management Science* 19, no. 12 (August 1973), pp. 1461–1462.

"Income and Substitution Effects in the Linder Theorem." *Quarterly Journal of Economics* 87, no. 4 (November 1973), pp. 629–633.

"Competitive Pricing and the Centralized Market Place." *Eastern Economic Journal* 1, no. 1 (January 1974), pp. 11–19.

"The Transformation of Values: What Marx `Really' Meant (An Interpretation)." *Journal of Economic Literature* XII, no. 1 (March 1974), pp. 51–62.

"The Graduated Work Incentive Experiment: An Overview of the Results on Consumption, Health and Social Behavior." *Journal of Human Resources* IX, no. 2 (Spring 1974), pp. 253–264.

With Hilda Baumol. "What Ails the Fabulous Invalid? It's Not What You Think!" *The New York Times,* Arts and Leisure Section (June 2, 1974), pp. 1–22.

*Pamphlets*

*Business Morality and the Social Interest: Smith vs. Marx.* New York University, Center for Applied Economics, Discussion Paper, 1974, 8 pp.

*It Takes Two to Tango, or Sind 'Separable Externalities' Überhaupt Möglich?* New York University, Center for Applied Economics, Discussion Paper, 1974, 8 pp.

1972-1973

*Chapter in Book*

"The Dynamics of Urban Problems and Its Policy Implications." In Maurice Peston and Bernard Corry, eds., *Essays in Honor of Lord Robbins.* London: Weidenfield and Nicolson, 1972, pp. 380–393.

*Articles*

"On Taxation and the Control of Externalities." *American Economic Review* LXII, no. 3 (June 1972), pp. 307–322.

With David Bradford. "Detrimental Externalities and Non-Convexity of the Production Set." *Economica* (May 1972), pp. 160–176.

With Wallace Oates. "The Cost Disease of the Personal Services and the Quality of Life." *Skandinaviska Enskilda Banken Quarterly Review* 2 (1972), pp. 44–54.

"J. R. Hicks' Contribution to Economics." *Swedish Journal of Economics* 74 (1972), pp. 503–527.

With Alfred G. Walton. "Full Costing, Competition, and Regulatory Practice." *Yale Law Journal* 82, no. 4 (March 1973), pp. 639–655.

With P. Heim, B. G. Malkiel, and R. E. Quandt. "Efficiency of Corporate Investment: Reply." *Review of Economics and Statistics* 55, no. 1 (February 1973), pp. 128–131.

*Contribution to Conference Proceedings*
"Environmental Protection and Distribution of Incomes."
In *Problems of Environmental Economics*. Paris: OECD, 1972,
pp. 67–73.

1971–1972

*Book*
*Economic Theory and Operations Analysis*, 3rd ed. Englewood
Cliffs, N.J.: Prentice-Hall, 1972, 626 pp.

*Articles*
"Optimal Depreciation Policy: Pricing the Products of
Durable Assets." *Bell Journal of Economics and Management
Science* 2, no. 2 (Autumn 1971).

With David F. Bradford. (trans.) M. Boiteux, "On the Management of Public Monopolies Subject to Budgetary
Constraints." *Journal of Economic Theory* 3, no. 3 (September 1971).

With Alvin K. Klevorick. "Input Choices and Rate-of-Re-
turn Regulation: An Overview of the Discussion." Reprinted in *Cowles Foundation Paper no. 337*.

"Environmental Protection at Minimum Cost." *American
Journal of Economics and Sociology* 30, no. 4 (October 1971).

"Utility and Value." *Encyclopaedia Britannica*, 1971 ed.

"Environmental Protection, International Spillovers and
Trade." *Wicksell Lectures*, Stockholm, Sweden.

With David F. Bradford. "Optimal Taxes and Pricing: Reply." *American Economic Review* LXII, no. 1 (March 1972),
pp. 175–176.

"Macroeconomics of Unbalanced Growth: Reply." *American
Economic Review* LXII, no. 1 (March 1972), p. 150.

"Jacob Viner at Princeton." *Journal of Political Economy* 80, no. 1, (January–February 1972), pp. 12–15.

With Mary I. Oates. "On the Economics of the Theater in Renaissance London." *Swedish Journal of Economics* 74 (March 1972), pp. 136–160.

*Book Review*

Review of Tibor Scitovsky, *Welfare and Competition*. In *Economica*, n.s. XXXIX, no. 153 (February 1971), pp. 89–90.

1970–1971

*Book*

*Portfolio Theory: The Selection of Asset Combinations.* New York: McCaleb-Seiler, 1970, 32 pp.

*Articles*

With David Bradford. "Optimal Departures from Marginal Cost Pricing." *American Economic Review* LX (June 1970), pp. 265–283.

With Alvin Klevorick. "Input Choices and Rate of Return Regulation: An Overview of the Discussion." *Bell Journal of Economics and Management Science* 1, no. 2 (Autumn 1970), pp. 162–190.

With Peggy Heim, B. G. Malkiel, and R. E. Quandt. "Earnings Retention, New Capital, and the Growth of the Firm." *Review of Economics and Statistics* LII, no. 4 (November 1970), pp. 345–360.

"The Firm with Inelastic Demands." In W. A. Ellis, M. F. G. Scott, and J. N. Wolfe, eds., *Induction, Growth and Trade, Essays in Honour of Sir Roy Harrod*. Oxford: Clarendon Press, 1970, pp. 348–360.

"Enlightened Self-Interest and Corporate Philanthropy." In Committee for Economic Development, *A New Rationale for Corporate Social Policy*. New York, 1970, pp. 3–19.

With Wallace E. Oates. "The Use of Standards and Pricing for Protection of the Environment." *Swedish Journal of Economics* 73, no. 1 (March 1971), pp. 42–54.

With Maco Stewart. "On the Behavioral Theory of the Firm." In Robbin Marris and Adrian Woods, eds., *The Corporate Economy*. London: Macmillan, 1971, pp. 118–143.

"Economics of Athenian Drama." *Quarterly Journal of Economics* LXXXV, no. 3 (August 1971), 365–376.

With Wallace E. Oates and E. P. Howrey. "The Analysis of Public Policy in Dynamic Urban Models." *Journal of Political Economy* 79, no. 1, (Jan.–Feb. 1971), pp. 142–153.

"Les décisions multivariées dans la théorie de l'Oligopole." *Revue d'Économie Politique*, no. 2 (Mars–Avril 1971), pp. 171–188.

## Book Review

Review of James Buchanan, *Cost and Choice*. In *Journal of Economic Literature* VIII, no. 4 (December 1970), pp. 1210–1211.


### 1969–1970


## Book

*Economic Dynamics*, 3rd ed. New York: Macmillan, 1970, 472 pp.

## Articles

With Richard E. Quandt. "The Demand for Abstract Transport Modes: Some Hopes." *Journal of Regional Science* 9, no. 1 (1969), pp. 159–162.

"Some Approaches to Urban Problems." *2nd Annual Report of the Economic Policy Council*, Department of the Treasury of the State of New Jersey, June 1969, pp. 50–56.

"On the Discount Rate for Public Projects." In Joint

Economic Committee, *The Analysis and Evaluation of Public Expenditures: The PPB System*. Washington, D.C.: U.S. Government Printing Office, 1969, pp. 489–503.

"Mathematics in Economic Analysis." In T. L. Saaty and F. J. Weyl, *The Spirit and the Uses of the Mathematical Sciences*. New York: McGraw-Hill, 1969, pp. 246–262.

"Comment on the Comment." *American Economic Review* LIX, no. 4 (September 1969), p. 636.

"The Social Rate of Discount: Comment on the Comments." *American Economic Review* LIX, no. 5 (December 1969), p. 930.

"Thoughts on the Present State of Economic Theory." *Indian Economic Journal* XVI (July–September 1968), pp. 69–70.

With H. D. Vinod. "An Inventory Theoretic Model of Freight Transport Demand." *Management Science* 15, no. 7 (March 1970), pp. 413–421.

"Free Market in Brokerage?" *Barron's*, November 4, 1968, pp. 1, 10, 12.

"On the Discount Rate for Public Projects." In R. H. Haveman and Julius Margolis, *Public Expenditures and Policy Analysis*. Chicago: Markham, 1970, pp. 273–290.

## Book Review

Review of Douglas Vickers, *The Theory of the Firm: Production, Capital and Finance*. In *Journal of Economic Literature* VII, no. 2 (June 1969), pp. 428–429.

1968–1969

## Book

With Stephen M. Goldfeld, eds., *Precursors in Mathematical Economics: An Anthology*. London: London School of

Economics Series of Reprints of Scarce Works on Political Economy, no. 19 (1968), 389 pp.

*Chapters in Books*
"Reasonable Rules for Rate Regulation." In Almarin Phillips and O. E. Williamson, eds., *Prices: Issues in Theory, Practice and Public Policy.* Philadelphia: University of Pennsylvania Press (1968), pp. 101–123.
"Performance of the Firm and Performance of Its Stocks." In H. G. Manne, ed., *Economic Policy and the Regulation of Corporate Securities.* Washington, D.C.: American Enterprise Institute, 1969, pp. 127–141.

*Book Review*
Review of G. L. S. Shackle, *The Years of High Theory.* In *American Economic Review* LVIII, no. 3 (1968), pp. 565–566.

*Articles*
"Entrepreneurship in Economic Theory." *American Economic Review* LVIII, no. 2 (May 1968), pp. 64–71.
"Sales Maximization vs. Profit Maximization: Are They Consistent? Comment." *Western Economic Journal* VI, no. 3 (June 1968), p. 242.
With Peggy Heim. "On the Financial Prospects for Higher Education." *Bulletin, American Association of University Professors* 54, no. 2 (Summer 1968), pp. 182–241.
With M. L. Balinski. "The Dual in Nonlinear Programming and Its Economic Interpretation." *Review of Economic Studies* XXXV, no. 3 (July 1968), pp. 237–256.
"On the Social Rate of Discount." *American Economic Review* LVIII, no. 4 (September 1968), pp. 788–802.
"Comment." *American Economic Review* LVIII, no. 4 (September 1968), pp. 896–897.

1967–1968

*Book Review*

Review of I. M. D. Little and A. C. Rayner, *Higgledy Piggledy Growth Again.* In *Economica*, n.s., (August 1967), pp. 326–329.

*Articles*

"Macroeconomics of Unbalanced Growth: The Anatomy of Urban Crisis." *American Economic Review* LVII, no. 3 (June 1967), pp. 415–426.

With Peggy Heim. "Further Progress: The Economic Status of the Profession, 1966–67," *AAUP Bulletin* 53, no. 2 (June 1967), pp. 136–195.

"On the Appropriate Discount Rate for Evaluation of Public Projects." *Congressional Record*, U.S. Senate, September 26, 1967, pp. 13693–13696.

"Discussion" (Tax Policy and Business Investment). In American Enterprise Institute, *Fiscal Policy and Business Capital Formation.* Washington, D.C. (1967), pp. 37–42.

"Calculation of Optimal Product and Retailer Characteristics: The Abstract Product Approach." *Journal of Political Economy* 75, no. 5 (October 1967), pp. 450–461.

With Robert Bushnell. "Error Produced by Linearization in Mathematical Programming." *Econometrica* 35, nos. 3–4 (July–October 1967), pp. 447–471.

With Burton Malkiel. "The Firm's Optimal Debt–Equity Combination and the Cost of Capital." *Quarterly Journal of Economics* LXXXI, no. 4 (November 1967), pp. 547–578.

"Statics and Dynamics in Economics." *International Encyclopedia of the Social Sciences*, vol. 15. New York: Macmillan, Free Press (1968), pp. 169–177.

1966-1967

## Books

With William G. Bowen. *Performing Arts: The Economic Dilemma*, New York: Twentieth Century Fund, 1966, 582 pp.

*Business Behavior, Value and Growth*, rev. ed., New York: Harcourt, Brace and World, 1966, 159 pp.

## Chapters in Books

"Economic Models and Mathematics." In Sherman R. Krupp, ed., *The Structure of Economic Science*. Englewood Cliffs, N.J.: Prentice-Hall, 1966, pp. 88–101.

"The Escalated Economy and the Stimulating Effects of Inflation." In T. Bagiotti, ed., *Etudi in Onore Marco Fanno*, vol. II. Padua: Cedam (1966), pp. 96–104.

"The Ricardo Effect in the Point Input–Point Output Case." In Martin Shubik, ed., *Essays in Mathematical Economics in Honor of Oskar Morgenstern*. Princeton: Princeton University Press, 1966, pp. 191–196.

## Articles

With Peggy Heim. "The Economic Status of the Profession, 1965–66." *AAUP Bulletin* 52, no. 2 (June 1966), pp. 141–195.

"Mathematical Analysis of Portfolio Selection, Principles and Application." *Financial Analysts Journal* (September–October 1966), pp. 1–5.

"A Possible Tax Stimulus for Productivity." *The Financial Times*, London, August 4, 1966, pp. 10, 18.

With Peggy Heim. "Salary Structures in Public Junior Colleges Which Do Not Have the Usual Academic Ranks." *AAUP Bulletin* 52, no. 4 (December 1966), pp. 401–407.

With Richard E. Quandt. "The Demand for Abstract Transport Modes: Theory and Measurement." *Journal of Regional Science* 6, no. 2 (1966), pp. 13–26.
With Peggy Heim. "On Contracting with Publishers: Or What Every Author Should Know." *AAUP Bulletin* 53, no. 1 (March 1967), pp. 30–46.
With F. H. Knight. "Economics." *Encyclopaedia Britannica*, vol. 7, 1967 ed., pp. 937–943.

## Book Review

Review of Abram Bergson. *Essays in Normative Economics*. In *Journal of Political Economy* LXXIV, no. 4 (August 1966), pp. 410–411.

1965–1966

## Books

*Welfare Economics and the Theory of the State*, 2nd ed. Cambridge: Harvard University Press, 1965, 212 pp.
*The Stock Market and Economic Efficiency*. New York: Fordham University Press, 1965, 95 pp.

## Articles

"Informed Judgment, Rigorous Theory and Public Policy." *Southern Economic Journal* XXXII, no. 2 (October 1965), pp. 137–145.
With Burton G. Malkiel and Richard E. Quandt. "The Valuation of Convertible Securities." *Quarterly Journal of Economics* LXXX (February 1966), pp. 48–59.
"Entreprise et Société," *Économié Appliquée*. Paris: Presses Universitaires de France, 1965, pp. 211–222.
With Peggy Heim. "Economic Status of the Profession: Taking Stock." *AAUP Bulletin* (1964–1965), pp. 248–301.

New Introduction to *Welfare Economics and the Theory of the State (Welfare and the State Revisited)*, L.S.E. (University of London), G. Bell, 1965. Pub. by Richard Clay (Chaucer Press), Ltd., Bungay, Suffolk.

1964–1965

## Book

*Economic Theory and Operations Analysis*, 2nd ed. Englewood Cliffs: Prentice-Hall, 1965 (expanded), 606 pp.

## Articles

"External Economies and Second-Order Optimality Conditions." *American Economic Review* LIV (June 1964), pp. 358–372.

With Tibor Fabian. "Decomposition, Pricing for Decentralization and External Economies." *Management Science* II (September 1964), pp. 1–32.

With Richard E. Quandt and Harold Shapiro. "Oligopoly Theory and Retail Food Pricing." *Journal of Business* XXXVII, no. 4 (October 1964), pp. 346–363.

With William G. Bowen. "On the Performing Arts: The Anatomy of their Economic Problems." *American Economic Review* LV, no. 2 (May 1965), pp. 495–502.

With Richard E. Quandt. "Investment and Discount Rates Under Capital Rationing – A Programming Approach." *Economic Journal* LXXV (June 1965), 317–329.

## Book Review

Review of J. M. Culbertson, *Full Employment or Stagnation?* In *Journal of Political Economy* LXXII, no. 6 (November 1964), pp. 633–634.

118    *William J. Baumol Publications*

*Chapters in Books and Contributions to Proceedings*
"Company Goals, Growth and the Multiproduct Firm." In
Reavis Cox, Wroe Alderson, and Stanley J. Shapiro, eds.,
*Theory in Marketing.* Homewood, Ill.: American Market-
ing Association, Irwin, 1964, pp. 322–332.
"Models of Economic Competition." In Peter Langhoff, ed.,
*Models, Measurement and Marketing.* Englewood Cliffs:
Prentice-Hall, 1965, pp. 143–159.
With Peggy Heim. "Economic Status of the Profession."
*AAUP Bulletin* 50, no. 2 (June 1964), pp. 136–184.
With Peggy Heim. "Economic Status of the Profession."
*AAUP Bulletin* 49, no. 2 (June 1963), pp. 138–187.


1963–1964

*Books*
With Lester V. Chandler. *Politicas y Procesos Economicos*
(Spanish ed. of *Economic Processes and Policies*), A. D. Roa
and C. J. De la Torre, trans., Bogota, D. E.: Editiones
Universidad Javeriana, 1963, 706 pp.
*Dinamica Economica* (Spanish trans. of *Economic Dynamics*),
Jose G. Guasch, trans. Barcelona, Spain: Marcombo, 1964,
430 pp.

*Chapters in Books and Contributions to Proceedings*
"Toward the Construction of More Useful Models." In
A. R. Oxenfeldt, ed., *Models of Markets.* New York:
Columbia University Press, 1963, pp. 172–188.
With Richard E. Quandt. "Dual Prices and Competition."
In A. R. Oxenfeldt, ed., *Models of Markets.* New York:
Columbia University Press, 1963, pp. 237–264.
"Urban Services: Interactions of Public and Private Deci-
sions." In Howard G. Schaller, ed., *Public Expenditure*

*Decisions in the Urban Community.* Washington, D.C.: Resources for the Future, 1963, pp. 1–18.

"Linear and Integer Programming." In *Proceedings of a Symposium on Decision Theory.* Division of Research, College of Business Administration, Ohio University, Athens, 1964, pp. 10–21.

## Articles

"An Expected Gain-Confidence Limit Criterion for Portfolio Selection." *Management Science* 10, no. 2 (October 1963), pp. 174–182.

With Richard E. Quandt. "Rules of Thumb and Optimally Imperfect Decisions." *American Economic Review* LIV (March 1964), pp. 23–46.

"Monopolistic Competition and Welfare Economics." *American Economic Review* LIV, no. 3 (May 1964), pp. 44–52.

## Book Review

Review of R. M. Cyert and J. G. March, *A Behavioral Theory of the Firm.* In *Journal of Marketing Research* 1 (February 1964), pp. 74–76.

### 1962–1963

## Books

*Théorie Économique et Analyse Opérationnelle* (trans. of *Economic Theory and Operations Analysis.* Paris: Dunod, 1963, 473 pp.

Japanese trans. *Business Behavior, Value and Growth.* Tokyo, 1963.

## Chapters in Books

(Reprint) "The Revenue Maximization Hypothesis." M. L. Joseph, N. C. Seeber, and G. L. Bach, eds., in *Economic*

*Analysis and Policy: Background Readings for Current Issues.* Englewood Cliffs: Prentice-Hall, 1963, pp. 220–226.

With Charles Sevin. (reprint) "Marketing Costs and Mathematical Programming." Edward C. Bursk and John F. Chapman, eds. In *New Decision-Making Tools for Managers.* Cambridge: Harvard University Press, 1963, pp. 237–265.

"Prerequisites for Economic Growth." From Hearings before Joint Economic Committee (Part 9a, 1959, pp. 2792–2796). In R. E. Slesinger and Asher Isaacs, eds., *Contemporary Economics.* Boston: Allyn and Bacon, 1963, pp. 239–242.

"From Problem to Model to Computer to Solution." In Wroe Alderson and Stanley J. Shapiro, eds., *Marketing and the Computer.* Englewood Cliffs: Prentice-Hall, 1963, pp. 202–217.

*Articles*

"On Dividend Policy and Market Imperfection." *Journal of Business* XXXVI (January 1963), pp. 112–115.

"The Theory of Expansion of the Firm." *American Economic Review* LII (December 1962), pp. 1078–1087.

"Annual Report by Committee Z." *AAUP Bulletin* 48 (Summer 1962), pp. 116–119.

With Peggy Heim. "The Economic Status of the Profession, 1961–62." *AAUP Bulletin* 48 (Summer 1962), pp. 120–154.

"On the Fringe: Retirement Contributions and Other Faculty Benefits." *AAUP Bulletin* 48 (December 1962), pp. 346–358.

1961–1962

*Book Reviews*

Review of Nicholas Kaldor, *Essays in Value and Distribution* and *Essays on Economic Stability and Growth.* In *American Economic Review* LI, no. 2 (June 1961), pp. 409–413.

Review of A. Charnes and W. W. Cooper, *Management Models and Industrial Application of Linear Programming*, vol. I. In *Naval Research Logistics Quarterly* 9, no. 1 (March 1962), pp. 63–64.

*Articles*

"Physical Distribution Systems: Discussion," in *The Social Responsibilities of Marketing*. In *American Marketing Association Proceedings*, 1962, pp. 525–526.

"Reappraisal of the Doctrine of Consumers' Sovereignty – Discussion." In *American Economic Review* LII, no. 2 (May 1962), pp. 288–290.

With Edward A. Ide (reprint) "Variety of Retailing." In Bass, Bussell, Greene, Lazar, Pessemier, Shawver, Schuchman, Theodore, and Wilson, eds., *Mathematical Models and Methods in Marketing*. Homewood, Ill.: Irwin, 1961, pp. 128–138.

(Reprint) "What Can Economic Theory Contribute to Managerial Economics?" In *The Executive* 5, no. 3 (August 1961), pp. 23–25.

"The Economic Status of the Profession, 1960–61." *AAUP Bulletin* 47, no. 2 (June 1961), pp. 101–114.

"Stocks, Flows and Monetary Theory." *Quarterly Journal of Economics* LXXVI (February 1962), pp. 46–56.

With Harold W. Kuhn. "An Approximative Algorithm for the Fixed Charges Transportation Problem." *Naval Research Logistics Quarterly* 9, no. 1 (March 1962), pp. 1–15.


1960–1961

*Books*

*Economic Theory and Operations Analysis*. Englewood Cliffs: Prentice-Hall, 1961, 438 pp.

With Klaus Knorr. *What Price Economic Growth?* Englewood Cliffs: Prentice-Hall, 1961, 174 pp.

## Articles

With Gary S. Becker. Revision and new postscript, "The Classical Monetary Theory: The Outcome of the Discussion." In Joseph J. Spengler and William R. Allen, eds., *Essays in Economic Thought: Aristotle to Marshall.* Chicago: Rand McNally, 1960.

With Ralph E. Gomory. "Integer Programming and Pricing." *Econometrica* 28, no. 3 (July 1960), pp. 521–550.

"Comment." In Universities National Bureau of Economic Research, *Demographic and Economic Change in Developed Countries.* Princeton: Princeton University Press, 1960, pp. 374–376.

"Monetary and Value Theory: Comments." *Review of Economic Studies* XXVIII, no. 75 (October 1960), pp. 29–32.

"Pitfalls in Contracyclical Policies: Some Tools and Results." *Review of Economics and Statistics* XLIII, no. 1 (February 1961), pp. 21–26.

"Mathematical Models and Thinking in Marketing." In American Marketing Association, *Proceedings of the 1960 Winter Conference.* Chicago, 1961, pp. 43–46.

"Economic Theory and the Marketing Curriculum." In American Marketing Association, *Proceedings of the 1960 Winter Conference,* Chicago, 1961, pp. 259–264.

"What Can Economic Theory Contribute to Managerial Economics?" *American Economic Review* LI, no. 2 (May 1961), pp. 142–146.

"Proposals for Increasing the Rate of Growth of National Output." In *What Price Economic Growth?* Englewood Cliffs: Prentice-Hall, 1961, pp. 30–47.

"The Appropriate Rate of Growth of National Output." In *What Price Economic Growth?* pp. 143–153.

## Book Reviews

Review of Edward S. Mason, ed., *The Corporation in Modern Society*. In *Journal of Political Economy* LXIX, no. 1 (February 1960), pp. 74–75.

Review of William Pfouts, *Essays in Economics and Econometrics: A Volume in Honor of Harold Hotelling*. In *Southern Economic Journal* XXVII (April 1961), no. 4, pp. 363–364.

### 1958–1959

## Books

*Economic Dynamics*, 2nd ed., New York: Macmillan, 1959, 396 pp.

*Business Behavior, Value and Growth*. New York: Macmillan, 1959, 164 pp.

## Book Reviews

Review of J. de V. Graaff, *Theoretical Welfare Economics*. In *Econometrica* 27 (April 1959), pp. 317–318.

Review of D. W. Bushaw and R. W. Clower, *Introduction to Mathematical Economics*. In *Econometrica* 28 (July 1959), pp. 512–513.

Review of K. J. Arrow, L. Hurwicz, and H. Uzawa, *Studies in Linear and Nonlinear Programming*. In *Kyklos*, fasc. 4 (1959), pp. 666–668.

## Articles

(Reprint) "On the Role of Marketing Theory." In Eugene J. Kelley and William Lazar, eds., *Managerial Marketing: Perspectives and Viewpoints*. Homewood, Ill.: Irwin, 1958.

"The Cardinal Utility Which Is Ordinal." *Economic Journal* LXVIII (December 1958), pp. 665–672.

"On Professor Neisser on Magnification." *Review of Economics and Statistics* LXI, no. 1 (February 1959), pp. 69–70.

"Orientation Toward Optimality in Business Planning." *Cost and Profit Outlook* XII (May 1959), p. 3.

"Reply" (to L. G. Telser's "A Theory of Speculation Relating Profitability and Stability"). *Review of Economics and Statistics* XLI (August 1959), pp. 301–302.

"Statement (on a Proposal to Increase Rate of Growth)," *Hearings, Joint Economic Committee of Congress*, Part 9a. Washington, D.C.: U.S. Government Printing Office, October 1959.

"Price Behavior, Stability and Growth." In *The Relationship of Prices to Economic Stability and Growth*. Washington, D.C.: U.S. Government Printing Office, March 1958.

With Philip Wolfe. "A Warehouse-Location Problem." *Operations Research* 6 (March–April 1958), pp. 252–263.

"Topology of Second Order Linear Difference Equations with Constant Coefficients." *Econometrica* 26 (April 1958).

"On the Theory of Oligopoly." *Economica* n.s. XXV (August 1958), pp. 187–198.

"Marginalism and the Demand for Cash in Light of Operations Research Experience." *Review of Economics and Statistics* XL (August 1958), pp. 209–214. (An earlier version appears in *Trends in Economics*, Second Conference of Pennsylvania Economists, Pennsylvania State University, 1958.)

"Activity Analysis in One Lesson." *American Economic Review* XLVIII (December 1958), pp. 837–873.

1957

*Articles*

"Operations Research Applied to Marketing Problems." *Cost and Profit Outlook* X (March 1957).

"A Guide to Operations Research Methods." *Cost and Profit Outlook* X (April 1957).

"On the Role of Marketing Theory." *Journal of Marketing* XXI (April 1957).

With Charles H. Sevin. "Marketing Costs and Mathematical Programming." *Harvard Business Review* 35 (September–October 1957).

"Interactions Between Successive Polling Results and Voting Intentions." *Public Opinion Quarterly* XXI (Summer 1957).

"Speculations, Profitability, and Stability." *Review of Economics and Statistics* XXXIX (August 1957).

"Cost Reduction Through Mathematical Programming." In *The Frontiers of Marketing Thought and Science*, American Marketing Association, 1957.

*Reviews*

Review of J. Tinbergen, *Economic Policy: Principles and Design*. In *American Economic Review* XLVII, no. 5 (September 1957), pp. 688–689.

Review of R. D. G. Allen, *Mathematical Economics*. In *Economica* XXIV (November 1957), pp. 364–366.

1956

*Articles*

"Acceleration without Magnification." *American Economic Review* XLVI (June 1956).

With Edward A. Ide. "Variety in Retailing." *Management Science* 3 (October 1956).

"Analyse Graphique de Modèles de Cycles Non Linéaires de Premier Ordre." In *Les Modèles Dynamiques en Économetrie*, Colloques Internationaux, LXII, Centre National de la Recherche Scientifique, Paris, 1956.

"Solution of Management Problems Through Mathematical Programming." *Cost and Profit Outlook* IX (May 1956).

With M. H. Peston. "More on the Multiplier Effects of a Balanced Budget: Reply." *American Economic Review* XLVI (March 1956).

"Consumer Information and Rational Choice." *Cost and Profit Outlook* IX (March 1956).

"Experimental Research in Consumer Behavior." *Cost and Profit Outlook* IX (February 1956).

*Review*

Review of F. Zeuthen, *Economic Theory and Method*. In *Journal of Political Economy* LXIV (December 1956).

1955

*Articles*

"Selecting an Appropriate Model for an Operations Research Problem." *Cost and Profit Outlook* VIII (November 1955).

With Maurice Peston. "More on the Multiplier Effects of a Balanced Budget." *American Economic Review* XLV (March 1955).

*Review*

Review of Leon Walras, *Elements of Pure Economics*, trans. by William Jaffe. In *Journal of Political Economy* LXIII (February 1955).

Review of Trygve Haavelmo, *A Study in the Theory of Economic Evolution*. In *Econometrica* 23 (July 1955).

1954

*Book*

With Lester V. Chandler. *Economic Processes and Policies*. New York: Harper, 1954.

*Articles*

"Professor Copeland's Study of Moneyflows." *Review of Economics and Statistics* XXXVI (February 1954).

"Economic Theory and the Political Scientist." *World Politics* VI (January 1954).

*Reviews*

Review of R. F. Harrod, *Economic Essays.* In *Econometrica* 22, (October 1954).

Review of Milton Friedman, *Essays in Positive Economics.* In *Review of Economics and Statistics* XXXVI (November 1954).

Review of B. S. Kierstead, *An Essay in the Theory of Profit and Income Distributors.* In *American Economic Review* XLIV (June 1954).

Review of John H. Williams, *Economic Stability in a Changing World* and *Trade Not Aid.* In *Review of Economics and Statistics* XXXVI (February 1954).

1953

*Articles*

"Discussion" (of papers at a session of the 1952 A.E.A. Annual meetings). *American Economic Review* XLIII (May 1953). Reprinted in *Three Papers on Recent Developments in Mathematical Economics and Econometrics*, Cowles Commission Papers n.s. no. 75.

"Firms with Limited Money Capital." *Kyklos* 6, art. 2 (1953).

*Review*

Review of Hansen and Clemence, eds., *Readings in Business Cycles and National Income.* In *Econometrica* 21 (October 1953).

1952

Book

*Welfare Economics and the Theory of the State.* London: Longmans Green, 1952.

Articles

With Gary S. Becker. "The Classical Monetary Theory: The Outcome of the Discussion." *Economica* n.s. XIX (November 1952).

"The Transactions Demand for Cash: An Inventory Theoretic Approach." *Quarterly Journal of Economics* LXVI (November 1952).

"Yet Another Note on the Harrod–Domar Model." *Economic Journal* LXII (June 1952).

Reviews

Review of Robert Dorfman, *Application of Linear Programming to the Theory of the Firm.* In *Journal of Political Economy* LX (October 1952).

Review of *International Economic Papers*, no. 1. In *Journal of Political Economy* LX (October 1952).

Review of J. S. Chipman, *The Theory of Inter-Sectoral Money Flows and Income Formation.* In *American Economic Review* XLII (September 1952).

Review of *Conference on Business Cycles.* In *Econometrica* 20 (April 1952).

Review of Kenneth J. Arrow, *Social Choice and Individual Values.* In *Econometrica* 20 (January 1952).

1951

Book

With Ralph Turvey. *Economic Dynamics.* New York: Macmillan, 1951.

*Articles*

Abstract of Discussion, "Recent Developments in Welfare Economics," by Tibor Scitovsky. *Econometrica* 19 (July 1951).

"The Neumann–Morgenstern Utility Index–An Ordinalist View." *Journal of Political Economy* LIX (February 1951).

1950

*Article*

With H. Makower. "The Analogy Between Producer and Consumer Equilibrium Analysis" (Part II of article, "Income Effect Substitution and Ricardo Effect"). *Economica* n.s. XVII (February 1950).

*Review*

Review of Jane Aubert, *La Courbe d'Offre*. In *Journal of Political Economy* LVIII (August 1950).

1949

*Articles*

"The Community Indifference Map: A Construction." *Review of Economic Studies* XVII (1949–50).

"Formalization of Mr. Harrod's Model." *Economic Journal* LIX (December 1949).

With Ralph Turvey, J. de V. Graaf, and G. L. S. Shackle. "Three Notes on Expectation in Economics." *Economica* n.s. XVI (November 1949).

"Relaying the Foundations." *Economica* n.s. XVI (May 1949).

1948

*Article*

"Notes on Some Dynamic Models." *Economic Journal* LVIII (December 1948).

1947

*Articles*

"Community Indifference." *Review of Economic Studies* XIV (1946–47).

"Notes on the Theory of Government Procurement." *Economica* n.s. XIV (February 1947).

*Reviews*

Review of Frank L. Kidner, *California Business Cycles*. In *Economica* n.s. XIV (May 1947).

Review of *Mathematics for Economists*. In *Economica* n.s. XIV (August 1947).

Review of F. C. Mills, *Price Quantity Interactions in Business Cycles*. In *Economica* XIV (November 1947).

# Index

Printed and bound by CPI Group (UK) Ltd, Croydon, CR0 4YY

16/04/2025